craft tree

Crocheted Baby Gifts

COMPILED BY **Amy Palmer**

INTERWEAVE
interweave.com

The projects in this collection were originally published in other Interweave publications, including Interweave Crochet, Interweave Knits, Knitscene, *and* Piecework *magazines and* CrochetMe *eBooks. Some have been altered to update information and/or conform to space limitations.*

Interweave Press LLC,
a division of F+W Media Inc
201 East Fourth Street
Loveland, CO 80537
interweave.com

Printed in the United States
by Versa Press

Table of Contents

Sir Stephen the Bunny

by Donna Childs

Antique toys were the inspiration for this cuddly stuffed rabbit. Each body part is crocheted separately in basic stitches. Vintage buttons provide embellishment and are used to join the arms and legs so the doll can be posed. Organic cotton yarn makes this a perfect gift for a recipient of any age.

Finished Size
About 16" (40.5 cm) tall with legs extended.

Yarn
Blue Sky Alpacas Organic Cotton (100% cotton; 150 yd [137 m]/3.5 oz [100 g]; (4)): #83 sage (MC), 2 skeins; #80 bone (A) and #82 nut (B), 1 skein each.

Hook
Sizes G/6 (4 mm) and I/9 (5.5 mm). Adjust hook size if necessary to obtain the correct gauge.

Notions
Fiberfill; yarn needle; two ½" (1.3 cm) shank buttons; four ⅞" (2.2 cm) 2-hole buttons; three ½" (1.3 cm) buttons; DMC pearl cotton size #5, color #223; 1 yd of ¾" (2 cm) wide ribbon.

Gauge
Rabbit: 15 sts and 7 rows = 4" (10 cm) in dc with smaller hook. Vest: 12 sts and 9 rows = 4" (10 cm) in dc/sc patt with larger hook.

notes

* If the toy is intended for a child three years old or younger, embroider features and sew pieces tog securely; do not use buttons or other embellishments that might pose a choking hazard.
* Head, body, arms, and legs are worked separately in rnds without turning. When fastening off each piece, leave a long tail for sewing.

Head

With smaller hook and MC, ch 4, sl st in first ch to form ring.

RND 1: Ch 3 (counts as dc here and throughout), 11 dc in ring, sl st in top of beg ch-3 to join—12 sts.

RND 2: Ch 3, 2 dc in each st around, dc in base of beg ch-3, sl st in top of beg ch-3 to join—24 sts.

RND 3: Ch 3, *dc in next st, 2 dc in next st; rep from * around, ending with dc in base of beg ch-3, sl st in top of beg ch-3 to join—36 sts.

RND 4: Ch 3, *dc in each of next 2 dc, 2 dc in next st; rep from * around, ending with dc in base of beg ch-3, sl st in top of beg ch-3 to join—48 sts.

RND 5: Ch 3, dc in each st around, sl st in top of beg ch-3 to join.

RND 6: Ch 3, dc in each of first 20 sts, 2 dc in each of next 6 sts for nose, dc in each of last 21 sts, sl st in top of beg ch-3 to join—54 sts.

RND 7: Ch 3, dc in each of first 20 sts, [dc2tog (see Glossary) over next 2 sts] 6 times, dc in each of last 21 sts, sl st in top of beg ch-3 to join—48 sts.

RND 8: Ch 3, dc in next st, dc2tog over next 2 sts, *dc in each of next 2 sts, dc2tog over next 2 sts; rep from * around, sl st in top of beg ch-3 to join—36 sts.

RND 9: Ch 3, *dc2tog over next 2 sts, dc in next st; rep from * to last 2 sts, dc2tog over last 2 sts, sl st in top of beg ch-3 to join—24 sts.

RND 10: Ch 3, *dc2tog over next 2 sts; rep from * to last st, yo, insert hook in next st, yo and pull up a lp, yo and draw through 2 lps on hook (2 lps rem on hook), insert hook in top of beg ch-3, yo and draw through ch and both lps on hook—12 sts. Fasten off and set aside (see Notes).

Body

With smaller hook and MC, ch 4, sl st in first ch to form ring.

RNDS 1–4: Rep Rnds 1–4 as for head—48 sts.

RNDS 5–12: Ch 3, dc in each st around, sl st in top of beg ch-3 to join.

RND 13: Ch 3, dc in next st, dc2tog over next 2 sts, *dc in each of next 2 sts, dc2tog over next 2 sts; rep from * around, sl st in top of beg ch-3 to join—36 sts.

RND 14: Rep Rnd 5.

RND 15: Ch 3, dc2tog over next 2 sts, *dc in next st, dc2tog over next 2 sts; rep from * around, sl st in top of beg ch-3 to join—24 sts.

RND 16: Ch 3, *dc2tog over next 2 sts; rep from * to last st, yo, insert hook in next st, yo and pull up a lp, yo and draw through 2 lps on hook (2 lps rem on hook), insert hook in top of beg ch-3, yo and draw through ch and both lps on hook—12 sts. Fasten off and set aside.

Arms (make 2)

With smaller hook and A, ch 4, sl st in first ch to form ring.

RND 1: Ch 3, 11 dc in ring, sl st in top of beg ch-3 to join—12 sts.

RND 2: Ch 3, 2 dc in next st and in each st around, dc in base of beg ch-3; changing to MC, sl st in top of beg ch-3 to join—24 sts.

RNDS 3–7: With MC, ch 3, dc in each st around, sl st in top of beg ch-3 to join.

RND 8: Ch 3, dc2tog over next 2 sts, dc in each of next 8 sts, [dc2tog over next 2 sts] 2 times, dc in each of next 8 sts, yo, insert hook in next st, yo and pull up a lp, yo and draw through 2 lps on hook (2 lps rem on hook), insert hook in top of beg ch-3, yo and draw through ch and both lps on hook, sl st in top of beg ch-3 to join—20 sts.

RND 9: Ch 3, dc2tog over next 2 sts, dc in each of next 6 sts, [dc2tog over next 2 sts] 2 times, dc in each of next 5 sts, yo, insert hook in next st, yo and pull up a lp, yo and draw through 2 lps on hook (2 lps rem on hook), insert hook in top of beg ch-3, yo and draw through ch and both lps on hook—16 sts. Fasten off.

Stuff and use yarn needle and tail to sew closed. Set aside.

Legs (make 2)

With smaller hook and MC, ch 4, sl st in first ch to form ring.

RNDS 1–7: Rep Rnds 1–7 as for arms—24 sts.

RND 8: Ch 3, dc in each of next 8 sts, 3 dc in each of next 6 sts, dc in each of last 9 sts, sl st in top of beg ch-3 to join—36 sts.

RND 9: Ch 3, dc in each st around, sl st in top of beg ch-3 to join. Fasten off.

Stuff but do not sew closed. Set aside.

Soles (make 2)

With smaller hook and A, ch 4, sl st in first ch to form ring.

RND 1: Ch 3, 11 dc in ring, sl st in top of beg ch-3 to join—12 sts.

RND 2: Ch 3, 2 dc in each st around, dc in base of beg ch-3, sl st in top of beg ch-3 to join—24 sts.

ROW 3: Ch 3, dc in each of next 7 sts, turn leaving rem sts unworked—8 sts rem.

ROW 4: Ch 3, dc2tog over next 2 sts, dc in each of next 2 sts, dc2tog over next 2 sts, dc in last st—6 sts. Fasten off.

Using yarn needle and tail from sole, sew a sole on bottom of each leg to close.

Ears (make 2)

With smaller hook and MC, ch 18.

ROW 1: (RS) Sc in bottom ridge lp of 2nd ch from hook and in bottom ridge lp of each ch across, turn—17 sts.

ROW 2: (WS) Ch 1, sc in each of first 17 sts, 3 sc in side of last sc of Row 1, turn work 180°, sc in both lps of each ch of foundation ch, turn—37 sts.

ROW 3: Ch 1, sc in each of first 18 sts, 3 sc in next st, sc in each of last 18 sts, turn—39 sts.

ROW 4: Ch 1, sc in each of first 19 sts, 3 sc in next st, sc in each of last 19 sts, turn—41 sts.

ROW 5: Ch 1, sc in each of first 20 sts, 3 sc in next st, sc in each of last 20 sts—43 sts.

Fasten off. Fold ear in half lengthwise with RS tog and whipstitch (see Glossary) from straight short end of ear along long edge for 2" (5 cm).

Vest

With larger hook and B, ch 46.

ROW 1: (WS) Sc in 2nd ch from hook and in each ch across, turn—45 sts.

ROW 2: (RS) Ch 3 (counts as dc), sk first st, dc in each st across, turn.

ROW 3: Ch 1, sc in each st across, turn.

ROWS 4–5: Rep Rows 2–3.

Right front

ROW 6: Ch 3, dc2tog over next 2 sts, dc in each of next 2 sts, dc2tog over next 2 sts, dc in next st, turn leaving rem sts unworked—6 sts.

ROW 7: Ch 1, sc in each st across, turn.

ROW 8: Ch 3, [dc2tog over next 2 sts] 2 times, dc in last st, turn—4 sts.

ROW 9: Rep Row 7—4 sts.

ROW 10: Ch 3, dc2tog over next 2 sts, dc in last st—3 sts. Fasten off.

Back

ROW 1: With RS facing, sk 8 sts of Row 5 and join yarn with sl st in 9th st, ch 3, dc2tog over next 2 sts, dc in each of next 7 sts, dc2tog over next 2 sts, dc in next st, turn—11 sts.

ROW 2: Ch 1, sc in each st across, turn—11 sts.

ROW 3: Ch 3, dc2tog over next 3 sts, dc in each of next 5 sts, dc2tog over next 2 sts, dc in last st, turn—9 sts.

ROW 4: Rep Row 2.

ROW 5: Ch 3, dc in each st across.

Fasten off.

Left front

ROW 1: With RS facing, sk 8 sts of Row 5 of vest base and join yarn with sl st in 9th st, ch 3, dc2tog over next 2 sts, dc in next 2 sts, dc2tog over next 2 sts, dc in last st, turn—6 sts.

Rep Rows 7–10 of right front. Fasten off. With yarn needle and B, sew shoulders. Join B with sl st at left underarm, sc evenly around armhole. Rep for right armhole. Sc evenly around outside edge of vest. Sew three ½" (1.3 cm) buttons on right front.

Finishing

Stuff body and head. Using pearl cotton, pass yarn needle from left side of body near neck edge through to right side and through first arm, through 1 hole of 2-hole button, back through other hole of button, back through arm, back through right side of body, and back through left side of body.

Cont through left arm and first hole, then 2nd hole of 2-hole button and back through left arm. You will have the 2 ends of the cord between the left arm and left side of body. Pull tightly to shape body and tie a secure knot. Attach the legs in the same way.

On head, sew shank buttons on either side of nose with pearl cotton, pulling the ends tog from inside of head to shape the face. Embroider nose and mouth with pearl cotton. Sew ears to either side of head, tilting them back at an angle. Sew head to body, adding a little more stuffing as you go so the head stands firmly. Weave in loose ends. Put the vest on the bunny and tie ribbon in a bow around his neck.

DONNA CHILDS began designing and crocheting clothes for her dolls when she was ten years old. She has loved playing with yarn ever since.

Snuggly HOODIE

by Lisa Naskrent

This hoodie by Lisa Naskrent is a great spring layer for the stylish baby, with a roomy hood and wide armholes that easily fit over an underlayer. The Shepherd Sock yarn is warm and, more importantly, washable.

Finished Size
21½ (23, 24, 25)" (54.5 [58.5, 61, 63.5] cm) chest circumference, 12½ (13½, 14½, 15½)" (31.5 [34.5, 37, 39.5] cm) length to fit 12 months (18 months, 2T, 3T). Garment shown fits 18 months.

Yarn
Lorna's Laces Shepherd Sock (80% superwash wool, 20% nylon; 215 yd [197 m]/2 oz [57 g]; (1)): #51ns island blue (MC), 5 (5, 6, 6) hanks and #608 ashburn (CC), 1 hank.

Hook
Size H/8 (5 mm). Adjust hook size if necessary to obtain correct gauge.

Notions
Stitch markers (m); yarn needle; four ¾" (2 cm) buttons.

Gauge
7 ch-2 sps and 14 rows = 4" (10 cm) in main body patt.

notes

* Garment is worked holding 2 strands tog throughout. Garment body is worked from the top down with hood completed last.

stitch guide

Sh
(Sc, ch 2, sc) in st indicated.

Beg double sh (beg-dbl-sh)
(Dc, [ch 2, sc] 2 times) in st indicated (counts as 2 ch-2 sps).

Ending double shell (end-dbl-sh)
([Sc, ch 2] 2 times, dc) all in st indicated (counts as 2 ch-2 sps).

Main body patt (multiple of 3 ch + 2)
Set-up row: Sh (see above) in 2nd ch from hook, [sk next 2 ch, sh in next ch] across, turn.

Row 1: Ch 1, sh in each ch-2 sp across, turn.

Row 2: Ch 1, beg-dbl-sh (see above) in first ch-2 sp, sh in each ch-2 sp to last ch-2 sp, end-dbl-sh (see above) in last ch-2 sp, turn.

Row 3: Ch 1, beg-dbl-sh in first ch-2 sp, sh in each ch-2 sp across, turn.

Row 4: Ch 1, sh in first ch-2 sp and in each ch-2 sp to last ch-2 sp, end-dbl-sh in last ch-2 sp, turn.

Note: Work set-up row and then rep Row 1 only for gauge swatch.

Back

With MC, ch 38 (41, 41, 44).

ROW 1: (RS) Work main body patt set-up row (see Stitch Guide), place marker (pm) in foundation ch (previous row) of 3rd ch-2 sp to mark left shoulder, pm in last ch-2 sp of foundation ch (previous row) to mark right shoulder, turn—13 (14, 14, 15) ch-2 sps.

ROWS 2–11 (13, 15, 15): Rep Row 1 of main body patt.

ROWS 12–15 (14–17, 16–19, 16–19): [Work (Row 2, Row 1) of main body patt] 2 times—17 (18, 18, 19) ch-2 sps. Fasten off.

Left shoulder and front

ROW 1: With RS facing, join MC in marked ch-2 sp for left shoulder, ch 1, sh in same ch-2 sp and in next 2 ch-2 sps, turn—3 ch-2 sps.

ROWS 2–5: [Work (Row 4, Row 3) of main body patt] 1 (2, 2, 2) times; **SIZE 12 MONTHS ONLY:** work (Row 4, Row 1) of main body patt; **ALL SIZES:** mark first ch-2 sp of Row 5 for hood—6 (7, 7, 7) ch-2 sps.

ROWS 6–10 (12, 14, 14): Rep Row 1 of main body patt.

ROWS 11–15 (13–17, 15–19, 15–19): [Work (Row 1, Row 3) of main body patt] 2 times, rep Row 1—8 (9, 9, 9) ch-2 sps. Fasten off

Right shoulder and front

ROW 1: With RS facing, join MC in marked ch-2 sp for right shoulder, ch 1, sh in same ch-2 sp and next 2 ch-2 sps, turn—3 ch-2 sps.

ROWS 2–7: [Work (Row 3, Row 4) of main body patt] 2 (3, 3, 3) times; **SIZE 12 MONTHS ONLY:** work (Row 4, Row 1) of main body patt, **ALL SIZES:** mark last ch-2 sp in Row 5 for hood—8 (9, 9, 9) ch-2 sps.

ROWS 8–10 (12, 14, 14): Work Row 1 of main body patt.

ROWS 11–15 (13–17, 15–19, 15–19): [Work (Row 1, Row 4) of main body patt] 2 times, rep Row 1, do not fasten off—10 (11, 11, 11) ch-2 sps.

Joining panels

ROW 1: (WS) Ch 1, sh in each ch-2 sp across right front, ch 8 (8, 11, 11), sh in first ch-2 sp of last row on WS of back and in each ch-2 sp across, ch 8 (8, 11, 11), sh in first ch-2 sp of last row on WS of left front and in each ch-2 sp across, turn—35 (38, 38, 39) ch-2 sps.

ROW 2: Ch 1, sh in first 8 (9, 9, 9) ch-2 sps, *[sk next 2 ch, sh in next ch] 2 (2, 3, 3) times, sk next 2 ch*, sh in next 17 (18, 18, 19) ch-2 sps, rep from * to *, sh in last 10 (11, 11, 11) ch-2 sps, turn—39 (42, 44, 45) ch-2 sps.

Work Row 1 of main body patt until piece measures 12 (13, 14, 15)" (30.5 [33, 35.5, 38] cm). Fasten off.

Armholes

With RS facing, join MC with sl st to left underarm.

RND 1: Ch 1, work 34 (38, 44, 44) sc evenly in row-ends around armhole, with CC, sl st in first sc to join.

RND 2: Ch 1, sc around, sl st in first sc to join.

RND 3: Ch 1, rev sc (see Glossary) around, sl st in first rev sc to join. Fasten off.

Rep for right armhole.

Hood

ROW 1: With RS facing, join MC in row-end of first st marked for hood, work 10 sc evenly around neck to shoulder seam, work 27 (29, 31, 33) sc evenly around back of neck, work 10 sc down other side of front to next m, remove both m, turn—47 (49, 51, 53) sc.

ROW 2: Ch 1, sc across, turn.

ROW 3: Ch 1, 2 sc in first sc, sc to last sc, 2 sc in last sc, turn—49 (51, 53, 55) sc.

ROW 4: Rep Row 2.

ROW 5: Rep Row 3—51 (53, 55, 57) sc.

ROW 6: Rep Row 2.

ROW 7: Ch 1, sh in first sc, [sk next sc, sh in next sc] 25 (26, 27, 28) times—26 (27, 28, 29) ch-2 sps.

Rep Row 1 of main body patt until hood measures 7½ (8, 8¼, 8¾)" (19 [20.5, 21, 22] cm) from Row 1. Fasten off.

Center of hood

Beg on opposite end from where fastened off, join MC to 10 (10, 10, 11)th ch-2 sp, ch 1, sh in same ch-2 sp and in next 7 (8, 9, 8) ch-2 sps, leave rem 9 (9, 9, 10) ch-2 sps unworked—8 (9,

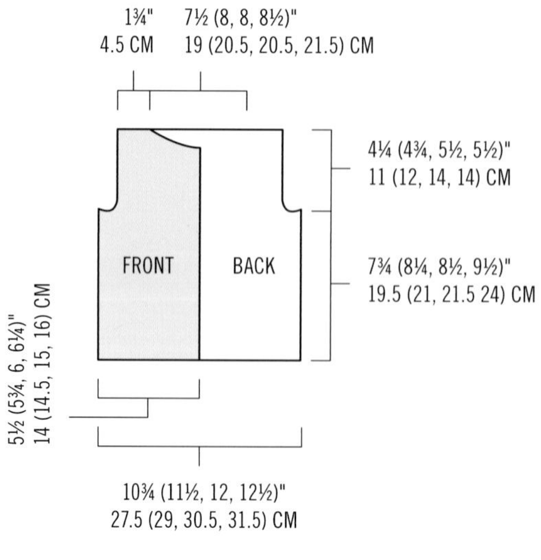

10, 9) ch-2 sps. Work Row 1 of main body patt until center piece measures 5 (5, 5, 5½)" (12.5 [12.5, 12.5, 14] cm). Fasten off. With RS facing, sl st seams of hood tog.

Finishing

Main edging

With RS facing, join MC to bottom corner of right front.

RND 1: Ch 1, work 37 (40, 43, 46) sc evenly up front to hood, work 5 sc evenly along row-ends of sc rows, work 1 sc in each row-end along hood to hood center, work 2 sc in each ch-2 sp across hood center, work 1 sc in each row-end along other side of hood to sc rows at bottom of hood, work 5 sc evenly along sc row-ends, mark last sc made for buttonholes, work 37 (40, 43, 46) sc evenly in row-ends down next panel, turn work 90 degrees, 3 sc in first ch-2 sp, pm in center sc to mark corner, work 2 sc in each ch-2 sp to last ch-2 sp, 2 sc in last ch-2 sp (corner), pm in last sc to mark corner, sl st in first sc to join.

RND 2: Ch 1, sc in each sc to hood, sc around hood working 6 sc2tog evenly spaced across, sc in rem sc to m, sc in same sc as m, sc in next 3 sc, ch 2, sk next sc, [sc in next 9 (10, 11, 12) sc, ch 2, sk next sc] 3 times, sc around working 3 sc at each corner and moving m up, with CC, sl st in first sc to join.

RND 3: Ch 1, sc around, working 1 sc in each ch-2 sp and 3 sc in each corner, sl st in first sc to join.

RND 4: Ch 1, rev sc around, sl st in first rev sc to join. Fasten off.

Pocket (make 2)

ROW 1: With MC, ch 11, work set-up row of main body patt—4 ch-2 sps.

ROWS 2–8: Work Row 1 of main body patt. Do not fasten off.

Pocket edging

RND 1: Ch 1, 3 sc in first ch-2 sp, pm in center sc to mark corner, 2 sc in each ch-2 sp to last ch-2 sp, 3 sc in last ch-2 sp, pm in center sc to mark corner, *rotate pocket 90°, work 8 sc evenly along row-ends of next side*, rotate pocket 90°, work 3 sc in corner, pm in center sc to mark corner, work 4 sc evenly across bottom to corner, work 3 sc in corner, pm in center sc to mark corner, rep from * to *, sl st in first sc to join.

RND 2: Ch 1, sc around working 3 sc in each corner and moving m up, with CC sl st in first sc to join.

RND 3: Ch 1, sc around working 3 sc in each corner, sl st in first sc to join.

RND 4: Rep Rnd 4 of main edging.

Stitching bet the 2 rows of rev sc, sew a pocket to each front. Stitch down sides and across bottom. Sew buttons on right front opposite buttonholes. Weave in loose ends.

LISA NASKRENT works full-time as a designer in Macomb, Illinois. View her work at www.crochetgarden.com.

Cupcake HATS

by Brenda K. B. Anderson

You'll eat up the variety of stitches—single crochet, shell stitch, post stitches—in this delicious crochet sampler. Top it with a simple cherry or sprinkles and a candle.

Finished Size
14 (16, 18)" (35.5 [40.5, 45.5] cm) in circumference. Size shown measures 18" (45.5 cm).

Yarn
Bernat Satin Sport (100% acrylic; 237 yd [217 m]/3 oz [85 g]; (3)): #03007 aran (MC); #03610 fun in the sun (CC1); #03445 bubblegum (CC2); #03705 rouge (CC3); 1 skein each.
Note: You can make two 18" (45.5 cm) hats out of one skein of each color.

Hook
Size G/6 (4 mm). Adjust hook size if necessary to obtain correct gauge.

Notions
6 st markers (m; 1 of these should be a different color from the rest); yarn needle; opaque seed beads or bugle beads for sprinkles (optional); sewing needle and thread (matching MC; optional—used only for sewing sprinkles); a small amount of polyester fiberfill (to stuff cherry or candle and flame).

Gauge
Rnds 1–10 = 4" (10 cm) diameter.

notes

* Hat is crocheted from top down in the rnd.
* Cherry or candle is made separately and attached to top of hat.

Frosting

Note: If you plan to make a candle for top of hat, leave a 16" (40.5 cm) beg yarn tail.

RND 1: With MC, make an adjustable lp (see Glossary), 6 sc in lp, pull yarn tail to close—6 sts.

RND 2: 2 sc in each st around—12 sts.

RND 3: [Sc in next st, 2 sc in next st] 6 times—18 sts.

RND 4: [2 sc in next st, sc in next 2 sts] 6 times—24 sts.

RND 5: [Sc in next 2 sts, 2 sc in next st, sc in next st] 6 times—30 sts.

RND 6: [Sc in next st, 2 sc in next st, sc in next 3 sts] 6 times, placing marker (pm) in 6th, 12th, 18th, 24th, 30th, and 36th sts (use contrasting m in 36th st to mark end of rnd)—36 sts. **Note:** M will help track inc and end of each rnd; move m up each rnd.

RND 7: [Sc in next 5 sts, 2 sc in next st] 6 times—42 sts.

RND 8: [Sc in next 3 sts, 2 sc in next st, sc in next 3 sts] 6 times—48 sts.

RND 9: [Sc in next 6 sts, 2 sc in next st, sc in next st] 6 times—54 sts.

RND 10: [2 sc in next st, sc in next 8 sts] 6 times—60 sts.

RND(S) 11 (11–12, 11–14): Work 1 (2, 4) rnds, inc 1 time bet each set of m. Make inc in a different place each rnd—66 (72, 84) sts. Remove first, 3rd, and 5th m.

RNDS 12–18 (13–20, 15–22): Work 6 (8, 8) rnds of sc, inc 1 time bet each set of m—84 (96, 108) sts. Remove all m except rnd m.

RNDS 19–20 (21–22, 23–24): Sc around.

RND 21 (23, 25) (SHELL RND): Sk first 2 sts, 4 dc flo in next st, sk next 2 sts, sc flo in next st, [sk next 2 sts, 4 dc flo in next st, sk next 2 sts, sc flo in next st,] 12 (14, 16) times, sk next 2 sts, 4 dc flo in next st, sk next 2 sts, sl st flo in last st. Fasten off leaving a 30" (76 cm) tail for sewing—14 (16, 18) shells.

Cake

RND 1: Working into unused back lps from previous rnd, join (CC1) with sl st in last st of previous rnd, ch 1, sc blo around—84 (96, 108) sts.

RNDS 2–4: Sc around—84 (96, 108) sts. Do not fasten off.

Cupcake Liner

Change to CC2 as foll: Insert hook in next st, yo with CC2 and draw through st and lp on hook. Sl st in each st around. Fasten off CC1—84 (96, 108) sts.

Note: Next rnd, work in sts from Rnd 4 of cake. Do not work into previous rnd of sl sts. Beg working in joined rnds.

Size 14" (35.5 cm) only

RND 1: Ch 3 (counts as dc throughout), dc2tog (see Glossary), dc in next st, dc2tog, [dc in next 4 sts, dc2tog] 6 times, [dc in next st, dc2tog] 2 times, [dc in next 4 sts, dc2tog] 6 times, sl st in top of beg ch-3 to join—68 sts.

Size 16" (40.5 cm) only

RND 1: Ch 3, dc2tog (see Glossary), dc in next st, dc2tog, [dc in next 4 sts, dc2tog,] 7 times, [dc in next st, dc2tog] 2 times, [dc in next 4 sts, dc2tog] 7 times, sl st in top of beg ch-3 to join—78 sts.

Size 18" (45.5 cm) only

RND 1: Ch 3, dc in next 2 sts, dc2tog (see Glossary), [dc in next 4 sts, dc2tog, dc in next 3 sts, dc2tog] 2 times, *dc in next 3 sts, dc2tog, [dc in next 4 sts, dc2tog, dc in next 3 sts, dc2tog] 2 times; rep from * 2 times, sl st in top of beg ch-3 to join—88 sts.

All sizes

RND 2: Ch 1 (counts as sc throughout), *FPdc (see Glossary) in next st, sc in next st; rep from * to last st, FPdc in last st, sl st in beg ch-1 to join—68 (78, 88) sts.

RND 3: Ch 1, FPdc in each FPdc, sc in each sc around, sl st in beg ch-1 to join—68 (78, 88) sts.

RNDS 4–8 (10, 12): Rep Rnd 3 five (seven, nine) times. Fasten off.

With MC, thread a piece of yarn 24" (61 cm) long onto yarn needle and tack down each sc bet each shell, and the center tip of each shell in the last row of frosting. This prevents scalloped edge from flipping up. In order to avoid long floats bet tack sts, weave yarn into a few sts bet tack sts inside of hat.

Cherry Stem

With CC3, and beg with a 16" (40.5 cm) yarn tail, ch 5, sl st in 2nd ch from hook, sl st in next 4 ch. Fasten off, leaving a 16" (40.5 cm) yarn tail.

Cherry

RND 1: With CC3, make an adjustable lp, 6 sc in lp, pull on beg yarn tail to close—6 sts.

RND 2: 2 sc in each st around, pm in first st of rnd to mark beg; move m up each rnd—12 sts.

RND 3: [Sc in next 2 sts, 2 sc in next st] 4 times—16 sts.

RNDS 4–5: Sc in each st around—16 sts.

RND 6: [Sc in next 2 sts, sc2tog (see Glossary)] 4 times—12 sts. Stuff cherry firmly with fiberfill.

RND 7: [Sc2tog] 6 times—6 sts.

Fasten off. Using yarn needle, thread yarn tail through the front lp of last 6 sts. Pull tight and weave in end.

To fasten cherry to hat

With yarn needle, poke each yarn tail from cherry stem through cherry (from top to bottom), and then through center top of hat. Tie yarn ends securely inside hat. Thread each yarn tail back up through to top of cherry (where stem comes out) and tie again. Rep as necessary to firmly secure cherry. Hide yarn ends inside cherry.

Candle

With CC3, ch 8, sl st in first ch to join.

RNDS 1–8: Sc around, pm in first st of rnd to mark beg; move m up each rnd—8 sts.

Fasten off, leaving a long tail for sewing.

Flame

With CC2, make an adjustable lp, 6 sc in lp, pull on beg yarn tail to close—6 sts.

RND 2: 2 sc in each st around; pm in first st of rnd—12 sts.

RNDS 3–4: Sc around.

RND 5: Sc in next 2 sts, sc2tog, sc in next 8 sts—11 sts.

RND 6: Sc in next 6 sts, sc2tog, sc in next 3 sts—10 sts. Stuff flame with polyester fiberfill.

RND 7: Sc in next 4 sts, sc2tog, sc in next 4 sts—9 sts.

RND 8: [Sc in next st, sc2tog] 3 times—6 sts.

RNDS 9–10: Sc around.

Fasten off, leaving a long tail for sewing.

To fasten candle and flame to hat

Using yarn needle, poke yarn tail through flame and out the bottom. Make one small st in bottom of flame to anchor yarn end, then feed through candle and through center top of hat. Rep with other yarn end of flame. Pull tails tightly enough to keep flame in place on top of candle. Stuff a small amount of fiberfill into candle to help keep its shape. Tie yarn ends from flame tog securely inside hat. Hide yarn tails inside candle. Use yarn tails from candle to sew bottom of candle to top of hat, and top of candle to bottom of flame. Hide ends inside candle.

Finishing

Weave in ends. Thread beg yarn tail from frosting onto yarn needle and push up through hat and out at base of candle. Wrap tightly around candle a few times and push back into candle near top edge of candle. Make a couple small sts in candle to secure end. Hide end inside candle.

With sewing needle and thread, sew beads to frosting.

BRENDA K. B. ANDERSON makes mascots during the day and lives in a little house in Saint Paul, Minnesota, with her awesome husband and their hairy baby, Mr. Kittypants.

Simply BIBS

by Lisa Naskrent

Lisa Naskrent creates two variations on a theme—both as simple as 1-2-3, A-B-C. Practice color-changing skills as you work these up, then make more with your own designs.

Finished Size
About 7¾" (19.5 cm) wide and 7" (18 cm) long.

Yarn
Mission Falls 1824 Cotton (100% cotton; 84 yd [77 m]/1.75 oz [50 g]; (3)):

Blocks bib: #207 chili (MC), #209 maize (A), #400 fog (B), #403 sky (C), 1 ball each.

Balloons bib: #103 pebble (MC), #300 lichen (A), #208 merlot (B), #201 coral (C), 1 ball each. Yarns distributed by CNS Yarns.

Hook
Size H/8 (5 mm). Adjust hook size if necessary to obtain correct gauge.

Notions
Yarn needle; 1 stitch marker (m); one ¾" (2 cm) button.

Gauge
13 sts and 15 rows = 4" (10 cm) in sc.

notes

* The yarn shown is no longer available. Substitute the DK-weight (3) yarn of your choice.
* Work colors according to charts. Each square represents 1 sc. To change colors, pull new color through last 2 lps on hook of last st and drop old color. Do not crochet over or fasten off until color is not used in subsequent rows. Pick up new colors on WS rows.
* Button is fastened in outer buttonholes to be adjustable. Do not leave child unattended with bib as button could be choking hazard.

Bib

With MC, ch 20.

ROW 1: (RS) Sc in 2nd ch from hook and in each ch across, turn—19 sc.

ROWS 2–3: Ch 1, 2 sc in first sc, sc to last sc, 2 sc in last sc, turn—23 sc.

Blocks bib only

ROWS 4–20: Ch 1, sc across foll colorwork on indicated rows of chart, turn.

ROWS 21–22: Ch 1, with MC sc across, turn.

Balloons bib only

ROWS 4–10: Ch 1, sc across, turn.

ROWS 11–22: Rep Row 4, foll colorwork on indicated rows of chart.

Both bibs

ROW 23: Ch 1, sc across, place marker (pm) in 6th sc to mark beg of second band. Do not fasten off.

Neckband

First band

ROW 1: Ch 1, sc in first 6 sc, leave rem sts unworked, turn—6 sc.

ROW 2: Ch 1, sc2tog (see Glossary), sc across, turn—5 sc.

ROW 3: Ch 1, sc in first 3 sc, sc2tog, turn—4 sc.

ROW 4: Rep Row 2—3 sc.

ROWS 5–14: Ch 1, sc across, turn.

ROW 15: Ch 1, sc in first sc, ch 1, sk next sc, sc in last sc, turn—2 sc.

ROW 16: Ch 1, sc in first sc, sc in next ch-1 sp, sc in last sc, turn—3 sc.

ROW 17: Ch 1, sc2tog, 2 sc in next sc, turn.

ROW 18: Ch 1, 2 sc in first sc, sc2tog, turn.

ROWS 19–22: Rep Rows 15–18.

ROWS 23–24: Rep Rows 15–16. Fasten off.

Second band

ROW 1: With WS facing, join MC in marked sc, ch 1, sc in same sc and in next 5 sc, turn—6 sc. **Note:** Unworked sts bet bands will be referred to as neckline in edging.

ROW 2: (RS) Ch 1, sc in each sc to last 2 sc, sc2tog, turn—5 sc.

ROW 3: Ch 1, sc2tog, sc across, turn—4 sc.

ROW 4: Rep Row 2—3 sc.

ROWS 5–16: Ch 1, sc across, turn.

BALLOONS

A Lichen #300 | B Merlot #208 | C Coral #201 | MC Pebble #103

MC	MC	MC	MC	MC	MC	MC	MC	MC	MC	MC	MC	MC	MC	MC	MC	MC	MC	MC	MC	MC	MC	MC	
MC	MC	MC	MC	MC	MC	MC	MC	MC	MC	A	A	A	MC	MC	MC	MC	MC	MC	MC	MC	MC	MC	22
MC	MC	MC	MC	MC	MC	MC	MC	MC	A	A	A	A	A	MC	MC	MC	MC	MC	MC	MC	MC	MC	
MC	MC	MC	MC	MC	MC	MC	MC	A	A	A	A	A	A	A	MC	MC	MC	MC	MC	MC	MC	MC	20
MC	MC	MC	MC	MC	MC	MC	MC	A	A	A	A	A	A	A	MC	MC	MC	MC	MC	MC	MC	MC	
MC	MC	MC	MC	MC	C	C	C	A	A	A	A	A	A	A	B	B	B	MC	MC	MC	MC	MC	18
MC	MC	MC	MC	C	C	C	C	C	A	A	A	A	A	B	B	B	B	B	MC	MC	MC	MC	
MC	MC	MC	C	C	C	C	C	C	C	A	A	A	B	B	B	B	B	B	B	MC	MC	MC	16
MC	MC	MC	C	C	C	C	C	C	C	A	A	A	B	B	B	B	B	B	B	MC	MC	MC	
MC	MC	MC	C	C	C	C	C	C	C	MC	MC	MC	B	B	B	B	B	B	B	MC	MC	MC	14
MC	MC	MC	C	C	C	C	C	C	C	MC	MC	MC	B	B	B	B	B	B	B	MC	MC	MC	
MC	MC	MC	MC	C	C	C	C	C	MC	MC	MC	MC	MC	B	B	B	B	B	MC	MC	MC	MC	12
MC	MC	MC	MC	MC	C	C	C	MC	MC	MC	MC	MC	MC	MC	B	B	B	MC	MC	MC	MC	MC	
MC	MC	MC	MC	MC	MC	MC	MC	MC	MC	MC	MC	MC	MC	MC	MC	MC	MC	MC	MC	MC	MC	MC	10

BLOCKS

A Maize #209 | B Fog #400 | C Sky #403 | MC Chili #207

MC	MC	MC	MC	MC	MC	MC	MC	MC	MC	MC	MC	MC	MC	MC	MC	MC	MC	MC	MC	MC	MC	MC	
MC	MC	MC	MC	MC	MC	MC	MC	MC	C	C	C	C	C	C	C	C	C	C	C	MC	MC	MC	20
MC	MC	MC	MC	MC	MC	MC	MC	MC	C	C	C	C	C	C	C	C	C	C	C	MC	MC	MC	
MC	MC	MC	MC	MC	MC	MC	MC	MC	C	C	C	C	C	C	C	C	C	C	C	MC	MC	MC	18
MC	MC	MC	MC	MC	MC	MC	MC	MC	C	C	C	C	C	C	C	C	C	C	C	MC	MC	MC	
MC	MC	MC	A	A	A	A	A	A	B	B	B	B	B	C	C	C	C	C	C	MC	MC	MC	16
MC	MC	MC	A	A	A	A	A	A	B	B	B	B	B	C	C	C	C	C	C	MC	MC	MC	
MC	MC	MC	A	A	A	A	A	A	B	B	B	B	B	C	C	C	C	C	C	MC	MC	MC	14
MC	MC	MC	A	A	A	A	A	A	B	B	B	B	B	C	C	C	C	C	C	MC	MC	MC	
MC	MC	MC	A	A	A	A	A	A	B	B	B	B	B	C	C	C	C	C	C	MC	MC	MC	12
MC	MC	MC	A	A	A	A	A	A	B	B	B	B	B	C	C	C	C	C	C	MC	MC	MC	
MC	MC	MC	A	A	A	A	A	A	B	B	B	B	B	C	C	C	C	C	C	MC	MC	MC	10
MC	MC	MC	A	A	A	A	A	A	A	A	A	A	A	MC	MC	MC	MC	MC	MC	MC	MC	MC	8
MC	MC	MC	A	A	A	A	A	A	A	A	A	A	A	MC	MC	MC	MC	MC	MC	MC	MC	MC	
MC	MC	MC	A	A	A	A	A	A	A	A	A	A	A	MC	MC	MC	MC	MC	MC	MC	MC	MC	6
MC	MC	MC	A	A	A	A	A	A	A	A	A	A	A	MC	MC	MC	MC	MC	MC	MC	MC	MC	
MC	MC	MC	MC	MC	MC	MC	MC	MC	MC	MC	MC	MC	MC	MC	MC	MC	MC	MC	MC	MC	MC	MC	4

ROW 17: Ch 1, 2 sc in first sc, sc2tog, turn.

ROW 18: Ch 1, sc2tog, 2 sc in last sc, turn.

ROW 19: Rep Row 5. Do not fasten off.

Edging

RND 1: (RS) With MC, ch 1, *3 sc in first sc, sc in next sc, 3 sc in next sc*, work 16 sc evenly in row-ends down first band to neckline, sc in each of next 11 neckline sc, work 21 sc evenly in row-ends up opposite band, at top of band, rep from * to *, work 42 sc evenly in row-ends down band and bib body to bottom ridge lps of foundation ch, 3 sc in first free bottom ridge lp, sc in each lp to last lp, 3 sc in last lp, work 39 sc evenly up body and band, changing to B in last st, sl st in first sc to join—166 sc.

RND 2: Ch 1, rev sc (see Glossary) in same sc and in each sc around, join with sl st to first st. Fasten off.

Finishing

With yarn needle and 2 strands of yarn, outline each square or circle in same color as square or circle using stem stitch embroidery (see Glossary). Work balloon strings in stem stitch. Using photo as a guide for colors, use stem stitch to embroider letters and numbers as desired. Sew button at end of 2nd band. Weave in all loose ends.

Molly's Mukluks

by Toni Rexroat

These super stylish booties are worked with full-fashion cables and a bootlike structure. Best of all, they stay on!

Finished Size
3½ (4, 4½, 5)" (9 [10, 11.5, 12.5] cm) long to fit newborn (3–6 months, 6–12 months, 18 months–2 years). Booties shown in size 3–6 months.

Yarn
Knit Picks Simply Cotton Worsted (100% cotton; 164 yd [150 m]/3.5 oz [100 g]; (4)): #C707 golden heather, 1 skein.

Hook
Size E/4 (3.5 mm). Adjust hook size if necessary to obtain correct gauge.

Notions
Four ⅝" (1.5 cm) buttons.

Gauge
8 sts and 4 rows = 2" (5 cm) in dc.

stitch guide

Tr2tog
*Yo 2 times, insert hook in indicated st and pull up lp, [yo and draw through 2 lps] 2 times; rep from *, yo and draw through all 3 lps on hook.

Even Moss Patt (multiple of 2 sts)
Row 1: Sk first ch (counts as hdc), sl st in next ch, *hdc in next ch, sl st in next ch; rep from * across.

Row 2: Ch 1 (counts as hdc), sk first st, *sl st in next hdc, hdc in next sl st; rep from * across.

Rep Row 2 for patt.

Quiver Patt (multiple of 4 sts + 3)
Note: Always work in ch st not in ch 1 sp.

Row 1: Ch 1 (does not count as st throughout), sc in first 3 sc, *ch 1, sk next sc, sc in next 3 sc; rep from * across, turn.

Row 2: Ch 1, hdc in first sc and in each sc and ch across, turn.

Row 3: Ch 1, sc in first hdc, tr in first skipped st from 2 rows below, sk next hdc, sc in next hdc, ch 1, sk next hdc, sc in next hdc, *tr2tog (see above) over previous skipped sc from 2 rows below and next skipped sc from 2 rows below, sk next hdc, sc in next hdc, ch 1, sk next hdc, sc in next hdc; rep from * to last 2 hdc, tr in previous skipped st from 2 rows below, sk next hdc, sc in last hdc, turn.

Rows 4–5: Rep Rows 2–3.

Rep Rows 2–5 for patt.

Sole (make 2)
Ch 9 (11, 13, 15).

RND 1: 3 dc in 2nd ch from hook, dc in next 6 (8, 10, 12) ch, 6 dc in last ch, rotate work; working in bottom ridge lp, dc in next 6 (8, 10, 12) ch, 3 dc in next ch, sl st in beg dc to join—24 (28, 32, 36) dc.

RND 2: Ch 2 (counts as dc), dc in first dc, 2 dc in next dc, dc in next 8 (10, 12, 14) dc, 2 dc in each of next 4 dc, dc in each dc to last 2 dc, 2 dc in each of last 2 dc—32 (36, 40, 44) dc. Fasten off and weave in ends.

Toe Cap (make 2)
Ch 9.

ROW 1: (RS) Sl st in 2nd ch from hook, *hdc in next ch, sl st in next ch; rep from * to last ch, hdc in last ch, turn—8 sts.

ROW 2: Ch 1, sl st in first hdc, *hdc in next sl st, sl st in next hdc; rep from * across, turn.

ROWS 3–6: Rep Row 2.

ROW 7: Rep Row 2, but do not turn, ch 23 (23, 27, 27), sl st in other end of row 7, being careful not to twist ch.

Shape sides
RND 1: (RS) Ch 1, beg Row 2 of even moss patt (see Stitch Guide): work 7 sts in row-ends down edge of toe cap, 7 sts in bottom ridge lps of toe cap, 7 sts in row-ends up opposite edge of toe cap, and in each ch, sl st in first st to join, place marker (pm) in sl st to mark beg of rnd, do not turn—44 (44, 48, 48) sts.

RNDS 2–6: Note: Beg working in a spiral without joining. Work in even moss patt.

Join sides to sole
With WS tog, pin sole and sides tog at middle of front and back and the middle of each side. Working through both thicknesses, sc sides and sole tog. **Note:** You will need to sc multiple sts from side to sole. Fasten off and weave in ends.

Right Bootie
ROW 1: (RS) With RS facing and toe to right, sk first 3 sts of opening from toe cap, join with sc in next bottom ridge lp of opening, sc in each bottom ridge lp around to toe cap, work 7 sc across toe cap, sc in bottom ridge lp of next 2 sts, esc (see Glossary) in last st, fsc 7 (see Glossary) for button tab—37 (37, 41, 41) sts. Fasten off.

ROW 2: With RS facing, join yarn in first st of opening, work Row 1 of quiver patt (see Stitch Guide) to last 2 sts, sc in last 2 sts, turn.

ROW 3 (BUTTONHOLE ROW): Ch 1, hdc in first 2 sts, ch 1, sk next st, hdc in next st, cont in Row 2 of quiver patt.

ROWS 4–6: Work Rows 3–5 of quiver patt always working 2 sts of button tab edge in sc or hdc.

ROW 7: Rep buttonhole row. Fasten off and weave in ends.

Left Bootie
ROW 1: (RS) Fsc 7 for button tab, with toe to left and RS facing, sc in 4th back ridge lp of opening from toe cap, sc in next 3 sts to toe cap, work 7 sc across toe cap, sc in bottom ridge lp of rem sts around. Fasten off and weave in ends.

ROW 2: With RS facing, join yarn in first st of button tab, ch 1 (does not count as st), sc in first 2 sc, work Row 2 of quiver patt.

ROW 3 (BUTTONHOLE ROW): Work Row 2 of quiver patt to last 4 sts, hdc in next st, ch 1, sk next st, hdc in next 2 sts, turn.

ROWS 4–6: Work Rows 3–5 of quiver patt always working 2 sts of button tab edge in sc or hdc.

ROW 7: Rep buttonhole row. Sew buttons opposite buttonholes.

TONI REXROAT is the editor of CrochetMe.com.

Pumpkin HAT

by Brenda K. B. Anderson

Worked vertically, this hat has enough stretch to fit a range of head sizes. The stuffed stem and curly leaf give this practical hat a great sense of humor.

Finished Size
14 (16, 18)" (35.5 [40.5, 45.5] cm) head circumference

Yarn
Plymouth Select Worsted Merino Superwash (100% merino; 218 yd [199 m]/3.5 oz [100 g]; (4)): #40 orange (MC), #41 teal (CC); 1 skein each.

Hook
Size G/6 (4 mm). Adjust hook size if necessary to obtain correct gauge.

Notions
Yarn needle; small amount of polyester fiberfill.

Gauge
16 sts and 9 rows = 4" (10 cm) in dc.

notes

* Body of hat is worked in rows. Crown is worked in spiral rnds after Row 41 (47, 53). Stem and leaf are worked separately and sewn on.

Pattern

With MC, ch 23 (26, 29), turn.

ROW 1: (RS) Sl st in 2nd ch from hook, sc in next ch, hdc in next 2 ch, dc in next 18 (21, 24) ch, turn—22 (25, 28) sts.

ROW 2: Ch 2 (counts as dc), sk first st, dc in next 17 (20, 23) sts, hdc in next 2 sts, sc in next st, sl st in last st, turn—22 (25, 28) sts.

ROW 3: Sl st in first st, sc in next st, hdc in next 2 sts, dc in next 18 (21, 24) sts, turn.

ROW 4: Rep Row 2.

ROW 5: Sl st blo in first st, sc blo in next 21 (24, 27) sts, turn.

ROW 6: Ch 1, sc blo in 2nd st from hook, sc blo in next 20 (23, 26) sts, sl st blo in last st, turn.

ROW 7: Rep Row 3.

ROW 8: Rep Row 2.

ROW 9: Rep Row 3.

ROW 10: Rep Row 2.

ROW 11: Rep Row 5.

ROW 12: Rep Row 6.

ROWS 13–36 (42, 48): Rep Rows 7–12 four (five, six) times.

ROWS 37–41 (47, 53): Rep Rows 7–11—7 (8, 9) sections.

Join first and last rows (to make a tube) as foll: With RS tog, line up foundation row directly behind last row made. Working through sts of both thicknesses, sl st in each st across through blo of last row made and foundation row. Do not fasten off.

Turn work RS out with sl st row-ends facing up.

RND 1: 3 sc in row-ends of each 7 (8, 9) sections of pumpkin—21 (24, 27) sc.

Size 14" (35.5 cm) only

RND 1: Sc in next st, sc2tog (see Glossary), 10 times—11 sts.

RND 2: Sc in next st, sc2tog 5 times—6 sts.

Size 16" (40.5 cm) only

RND 1: Sc2tog (see Glossary), 12 times—12 sts.

RND 2: Sc2tog 6 times—6 sts.

Size 18" (45.5 cm) only

RND 1: Sc in next st, sc2tog (see Glossary) 13 times—14 sts.

RND 2: Sc2tog 7 times—7 sts.

All sizes

Fasten off leaving a 10" (25.5 cm) tail. With yarn needle, thread tail through flo of rem 6 (6, 7) sts, pull tight to close top of hat. Weave in ends.

Stem

The stem is worked in a continuous top-down spiral.

RND 1: With CC, make an adjustable lp (see Glossary), 6 sc in ring, pull tail to close ring—6 sts.

RND 2: 2 sc in each st around—12 sts.

RND 3: [2 sc in next st, sc in next st] 6 times—18 sts.

Size 16" (40.5 cm) only

RND 4: [2 sc in next st, sc in next 5 sts] 3 times—21 sts.

Size 18" (45.5 cm) only

RND 4: [Sc in next st, 2 sc in next st, sc in next st] 6 times—24 sts.

All sizes

RND 4 (5, 5): Sc blo around—18 (21, 24) sts.

RND 5 (6, 6): Sc around—18 (21, 24) sts.

Size 14" (35.5 cm) only

RND 6: [Sc2tog, sc in next st] 6 times—12 sts.

RND 7: [Sc2tog, sc in next st] 4 times—8 sts.

Size 16" (40.5 cm) only

RND 7: [Sc in next 3 sts, sc2tog, sc in next 2 sts] 3 times—18 sts.

RND 8: [Sc2tog, sc in next st] 6 times—12 sts.

Size 18" (45.5 cm) only

RND 7: [Sc2tog, sc in next 2 sts] 6 times—18 sts.

RND 8: [Sc2tog, sc in next st] 6 times—12 sts.

All sizes

RND 8 (9, 9): Sc around—8 (12, 12) sts.

Sizes 16 (18)" (40.5 [45.5] cm) only

RNDS 10–11: Sc around.

Size 18" (45.5 cm) only

RNDS 12–13: Rep Row 10.

All sizes

RND 9 (12, 14): [Sc in next 3 sts, 2 sc in next st] 2 (3, 3) times—10, 15, 15 sts.

Size 14" (35.5 cm) only

RND 10: [Sc in next st, 3 sc in next st] 5 times—20 sts.

RND 11: Sc in next 2 sts, 4 sc in next st, [sc in next 3 sts, 4 sc in next st] 4 times, sc in next st—35 sts.

Sizes 16 (18)" (40.5 [45.5] cm) only

RND 13 (15): [Sc in next 2 sts, 3 sc in next st] 5 times—25 sts.

RND 14 (16): Sc in next 3 sts, 4 sc in next st, [sc in next 4 sts, 4 sc in next st] 4 times, sc in next st—40 sts.

All sizes

Fasten off, leaving a 12" (30.5 cm) tail. Stuff stem with fiberfill. Use yarn needle and yarn tail to sew stem onto center top of hat. Bury yarn tail in stem.

Leaf

Note: Leaf is worked in a spiral for 3 rnds, then back and forth for 2 rows.

RND 1: With CC, make an adjustable lp (see Glossary), 7 sc in ring—7 sts.

RND 2: 2 sc in each sc around—14 sts.

RND 3: 2 sc in each sc around, turn to beg working in rows—28 sts.

ROW 1: Ch 1 (does not count as st throughout),*[sc in next st, hdc in next st, 3 dc in next st, hdc in next st, sc in next st]** 2 times, sl st in next st, sc in next st, hdc in next st, [dc, 2 tr] in next st, [2 tr, dc] in next st, hdc in next st, sc in next st, sl st in next st; rep from * to ** 2 times, turn—40 sts.

ROW 2: Ch 1, sl st in next st, sc in next st, hdc in next st, 4 dc in next st, hdc in next st, sc in next st, sl st in next st, sc in next 3 sts, [hdc, dc, tr, dc] in next st, hdc in next st, sc in next 2 sts, sl st in next st, sc in next st, hdc in next 2 sts, dc in next st, [dc, 2 tr] in next st, ch 2, sl st in 2nd ch from hook (picot made; counts as 1 st), [2 tr, dc] in next st, dc in next st, hdc in next 2 sts, sc in next st, sl st in next st, sc in next 2 sts, hdc in next st, [dc, tr, dc, hdc] in next st, sc in next 3 sts, sl st in next st, sc in next st, hdc in next st, 4 dc in next st, hdc in next st, sc in next st, sl st in last st—53 sts.

Fasten off, leaving a 12" (30.5 cm) tail. With yarn needle and yarn tails, sew leaf onto hat near stem. Weave in ends.

Kiki DRESS

by Annette Petavy

Remember the classic Mondrian dress designed by Yves Saint Laurent in the 1960s? Here it is transformed into a child's tunic, and the original primary colors toned down one step to bright pastels. The front-loop-only single crochet keeps the fabric light while providing coverage.

Finished Size
22 (24, 26, 27½)" (56 [61, 66, 70] cm) bust circumference and 16¼ (19¾, 22½, 24¾)" (41.5 [50, 57, 63] cm) long to fit a child 2 (4, 6, 8) years old. Garment shown measures 22" (56 cm).

Yarn
Blue Moon Fiber Arts Sock Candy (96% cotton, 4% elite; 200 yd [183 m]/2 oz [57 g]; (2)): oats (A), 1 (2, 2, 2) skeins; chocolate (B), 1 (1, 2, 2) skeins; fuchsia (C), chamois (D), and dusty blue (E), 1 (1, 1, 1, 1) skein each.

Hook
Size E/4 (3.5 mm). Adjust hook size if necessary to obtain correct gauge.

Notions
Yarn needle.

Gauge
21 sts and 19 rows = 4" (10 cm) in sc flo.

notes

* Refer to schematic for color placement. Center 4 sts are always worked in B.
* For back, work color blocks in opposite color order of front.
* Entire garment is worked in sc front lp only (flo).

stitch guide

Dec row

Ch 1, sc2tog (see Glossary), sc flo to last 2 sts, sc2tog, turn.

Back

With B, ch 73 (79, 85, 89).

ROW 1: Sc flo in 2nd ch from hook and in each ch across, mark as RS, turn—72 (78, 84, 88) sts.

ROW 2: Ch 1, sc flo across, turn.

ROWS 3–4: Rep Row 2.

ROW 5 (BEG COLOR BLOCK): With A, ch 1, sc flo in first 34 (37, 40, 42) sts, with B, sc flo in next 4 sts, with C, sc flo in next 34 (37, 40, 42) sts, turn.

Working each st in same color as st in row below, rep Row 2 seven (eight, eight, ten) times. **Note:** First 8 (9, 9, 11) color-block rows completed. Foll schematic color diagram while working center 4 sts of every row in B, shape as foll: Work Dec row (see Stitch Guide)—70 (76, 82, 86) sts. Work dec row every 8 (9, 9, 11)th row 2 (3, 2, 4) times—66 (70, 78, 78) sts. Work Dec row every 6 (8, 8, 10)th row 4 (3, 5, 2) times—58 (64, 68, 74) sts.

With B, rep Row 2 three (three, four, four) times. Work even in top color-block colors according to diagram until work measures 11½ (14¼, 15½, 18)" (29 [36, 39.5, 45.5] cm). **Note:** If work already meets or exceeds this measurement, cont to shape armhole in top color-block colors:

Shape armhole

ROW 1: (RS) Sl st in first 6 sts, ch 1 (does not count as st), beg with next st sc flo to last 6 sts, turn leaving rem sts unworked—46 (52, 56, 62) sts.

ROWS 2–6: Work Dec row (see Stitch Guide)—36 (42, 46, 52) sts.

Work even in sc flo until armhole measures 5½ (6½, 7¾, 7¾)" (14 [16.5, 19.5, 19.5] cm) ending on a WS row, turn.

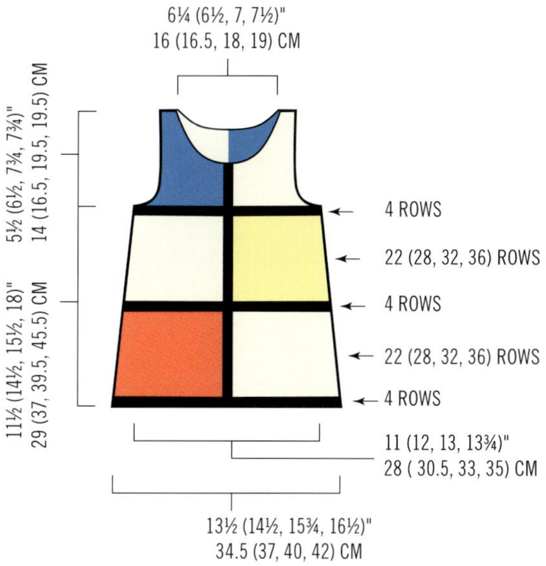

Shape back neck

(RS) Place marker (pm) in 30th (34th, 37th, 41st) st.

Right-back neck

ROW 1: Sc flo in first 6 (8, 9, 11) sts, turn leaving rem sts unworked—6 (8, 9, 11) sts.

ROWS 2–4: Ch 1, sc flo across working sc2tog flo at neck edge—3 (5, 6, 8) sts.

Work even in sc flo until armhole measures 5½ (6½, 7¾, 7¾)" (14 [16.5, 19.5, 19.5] cm). Fasten off.

Left-back neck

With RS facing, join yarn to m, remove m.

ROW 1: Ch 1, sc flo in next st, sc flo to end, turn—6 (8, 9, 11) sts.

Rep as for right-back neck, beg with Row 2.

Front

Work as for back through Row 6 of shape armhole. Work even in sc flo until armhole measures 5½ (6½, 7¾, 7¾)" (14 [16.5, 19.5, 19.5] cm), ending with a WS row—36 (42, 46, 52) sts.

Shape front neck

(RS) Pm in 23rd (26th, 29th, 32nd) st.

Right-front neck

ROW 1: (RS) Sc flo in first 12 (16, 17, 20) sts, turn leaving rem sts unworked—13 (16, 17, 20) sts.

ROW 2: Sl st in first 3 sts, ch 1, cont in sc flo to end—10 (13, 14, 17) sts.

ROW 3: Sc flo to last 2 sts, turn leaving rem sts unworked—8 (11, 12, 15) sts.

ROW 4: Sl st in first 2 sts, ch 1, cont in sc flo to end—6 (9, 10, 13) sts.

Cont in sc flo working sc2tog at neck edge every row 3 (4, 4, 5) times—3 (5, 6, 8) sts. Work even in sc flo patt until armhole measures 5½ (6½, 7¾, 7¾)" (14 [16.5, 19.5, 19.5] cm). Fasten off.

Left-front neck

ROW 1: Join yarn in marked st, remove m, sc flo in next st, sc flo to end—13 (16, 17, 20) sts.

ROW 2: Sc flo to last 3 sts, turn leaving rem sts unworked—10 (13, 14, 17) sts.

ROW 3: Sl st in first 2 sts, ch 1 (does not count as st), sc flo to end—8 (11, 12, 15) sts.

ROW 4: Work in est patt to last 2 sts, turn leaving rem sts unworked—6 (9, 10, 13) sts.

Cont in sc flo working sc2tog flo at neck edge every row 3 (4, 4, 5) times—3 (5, 6, 8) sts. Work even in sc flo patt until armhole measures 5½ (6½, 7¾, 7¾)" (14 [16.5, 19.5, 19.5] cm). Fasten off.

Finishing

Sew left-shoulder seam.

Neck edging

With RS facing, join B in first row-end at right shoulder, ch 1, working in sts and row-ends across back neck, across left-shoulder seam and across front, sc evenly around taking care that work remains flat, do not join, turn.

NEXT ROW: Ch 1, sc flo across, turn. Rep last row 2 times. With RS facing, sl st loosely around neck. Sew right-shoulder seam.

Armhole edgings

With RS facing, join B in any st at bottom of underarm, ch 1, working in sts and row-ends, sc evenly around, do not join, turn.

NEXT ROW: Ch 1, sc flo across, turn.

Rep last row 2 times. Sew side seams. Block to measurements.

ANNETTE PETAVY plays with yarn and colors in her home near Lyon, France. She blogs about her work and publishes patterns at www.annettepetavy.com.

Berry Baby HAT AND BOOTIES

by Chloe Nightingale

Adorable babywear hardly needs to be precious. This hat-and-booties pair are gender-neutral and sure to be well-worn and well-loved. The booties are perfect for first-time footwear makers; they're worked toe-up and the heel shaping is deceptively simple. The hat is topped with leaves to match those in the booties, and it's sized to fit even adults who enjoy embracing their inner whimsy.

Finished Size
Booties: 3¼ (4¼)" (8.5 [11] cm) long, to fit foot up to 3 (4)" (7.5 [10] cm). For ages newborn (1–3 months). *Hat:* 12 (14, 16, 19, 21, 23)" (30.5 [35.5, 40.5, 53.5, 58.5] cm) circumference at brim. For ages preemie (newborn, 0–3 months, 3–9 months, 9+ months/small child, larger child/adult).

Yarn
DK weight (Light #3), about 14 yd [13 m] in main color and 7 yd [6 m] in contrast color for booties; about 60 (85, 100, 136, 172, 204) yd (55 (78, 90, 125, 157, 187] m) in main color and 20 (60, 60, 60, 60, 60) yd (18 [55, 55, 55, 55] m) for hat.

Shown here: Rowan Pure Wool DK (100% wool, 136 yd [125 m]/1.75 oz [50 g], (3)): pomegranate 029 (red), less than 1 skein for booties and 1 (1, 1, 1, 2, 2) for hat, and glade 021 (green), less than 1 skein for booties and 1 skein for hat.

Hook
Size F/5 (3.75 mm). Adjust hook size if necessary to obtain the correct gauge.

Notions
Stitch marker (m); tapestry needle.

Gauge
18 sts and 22 rounds = 4" (10 cm) in sc.

notes

* Beg ch does not count as a st throughout patt.
* Booties, hat, and foliage are crocheted in a spiral without joining rnds. To help keep track of rounds, place a stitch marker (m) in the first st of the rnd to mark the beg of the rnd. Move m up as work progresses.

Booties

With red, ch 2.

RND 1: 5 sc in 2nd ch from hook, place marker (pm; see Notes) in first st, do not join—5 sts.

RND 2: 2 sc in each st around—10 sts.

RND 3: 2 sc in each st around—20 sts.

RNDS 4–10 (4–14): Sc in each st around.

RND 11 (15): Sc in each st around, turn.

Shape opening

ROW 1: Ch 1, sc in next 15 sts, turn leaving rem sts unworked—15 sts.

ROWS 2–6: Ch 1, sc in each st across, turn—15 sts.

Shape heel

ROW 1: Ch 1, sc in next 5 sts, sc2tog (see Glossary) over next 2 sts, sc in next st, sc2tog over next 2 sts, sc to end, turn—13 sts rem.

ROW 2: Ch 1, sc in next 4 sts, sc2tog over next 2 sts, sc in next st, sc2tog over next 2 sts, sc to end, turn—11 sts rem.

ROW 3: Ch 1, sc in next 4 sts, sc3tog (see Glossary) over next 3 sts, sc to end, turn—9 sts rem.

Fasten off, leaving a tail several inches long. Bring edges of last row together and, with tail threaded on a tapestry needle, use whipstitch (see Glossary) to sew back seam.

Leaf and top of bootie

Begin leaf

With green, ch 2.

ROW 1: 2 sc in second ch from hook, turn—2 sts.

ROW 2: Ch 1, 2 sc in each st across, turn—4 sts.

ROW 3: Ch 1, 2 sc in first st, sc in next 2 sts, 2 sc in next st, turn—6 sts.

ROWS 4–6: Ch 1, sc in each st across, turn.

ROW 7: Ch 1, sc2tog over first 2 sts, sc in next 2 sts, sc2tog over next 2 sts, turn—4 sts rem.

ROW 8: Ch 1, sc2tog over first 2 sts, sc2tog over next 2 sts, turn—2 sts rem.

ROW 9: Ch 1, sc2tog over rem 2 sts, turn—1 st rem.

Leaf edging

With yarn still attached, ch 1, work sc edging around leaf as foll: sc in end of each row, (sc, ch 1, sc) in tip of leaf, ch 1, do not fasten off—20 sc.

Bootie edging

With RS of bootie facing, join yarn and leaf with sl st to front right corner of bootie for one bootie and front left corner of bootie for the other. Ch 1, work 25 sc evenly around opening of bootie, working 1 sc in end of each row and in each of the 5 unworked sts from the toe-up section of the bootie, sl st in first sc to join.

RND 1: Ch 1 (counts as first hdc), hdc in each st around, sl st in beg ch-1 to join—25 sts.

RND 2: Ch 2 (counts as first dc), dc in each st around, sl st in top of beg ch-2 to join.

Fasten off and weave in loose ends.

Hat

With red, ch 2.

RND 1: 5 sc in 2nd ch from hook, place marker (pm; see Notes) in first st, do not join—5 sc.

RND 2: 2 sc in each st around—10 sc.

RND 3: 2 sc in each st around—20 sc.

RND 4: Sc in each st around.

RND 5: 2 sc in each st around—40 sc.

RNDS 6–7: Sc in each st around.

Preemie size only

RND 8: *2 sc in next st, sc in next 3 sts; rep from * around—50 sts.

RNDS 9–13: Sc in each st around.

RND 14: *2 sc in next st, sc in next 9 sts; rep from * around—55 sts.

RND 15: Sc in each st around.

Rep Rnd 15 ten more times or to desired length, sl st in next st. Fasten off.

Newborn size only

RND 8: *2 sc in next st, sc in next st; rep from * around—60 sts.

RNDS 9–14: Sc in each st around.

RND 15: *2 sc in next st, sc in next 11 sts; rep from * around—65 sts.

RND 16: Sc in each st around.

Rep Rnd 16 twelve more times or to desired length, sl st in next st. Fasten off.

0–3 month size only

RND 8: *2 sc in next st, sc in next st; rep from * around—60 sts.

RNDS 9–14: Sc in each st around.

RND 15: *2 sc in next st, sc in next 3 sts; rep from * around—75 sts.

RND 16: Sc in each st around.

Rep Rnd 16 fourteen more times or to desired length, sl st in next st. Fasten off.

3–9 month size only

RND 8: *2 sc in next st, sc in next st; rep from * around—60 sts.

RNDS 9–13: Sc in each st around.

RND 14: *2 sc in next st, sc in next 2 sts; rep from * around—80 sts.

RNDS 15–20: Sc in each st around.

RND 21: *2 sc in next st, sc in next 15 sts; rep from * around—85 sts.

RND 22: Sc in each st around.

Rep Rnd 22 twelve more times or to desired length, sl st in next st. Fasten off.

9+ month/child size only

RND 8: *2 sc in next st, sc in next st; rep from * around—60 sts.

RNDS 9–13: Sc in each st around.

RND 14: *2 sc in next st, sc in next st; rep from * around—90 sts.

RNDS 15–20: Sc in each st around.

RND 21: *2 sc in next st, sc in next 17 sts; rep from * around—95 sts.

RND 22: Sc in each st around.

Rep Rnd 22 sixteen more times or to desired length, sl st in next st. Fasten off.

Older child/adult size only

RND 8: *2 sc in next st, sc in next st; rep from * around—60 sts.

RNDS 9–13: Sc in each st around.

RND 14: *2 sc in next st, sc in next st; rep from * around—90 sts.

RNDS 15–20: Sc in each st around.

RND 21: *2 sc in next st, sc in next 5 sts; rep from * around—105 sts.

RND 22: Sc in each st around.

Rep Rnd 22 twenty more times or to desired length, sl st in next st. Fasten off.

Leaves

Preemie size only

With green, ch 2.

RND 1: 5 sc in 2nd ch from hook, pm in first st, do not join—5 sc.

RNDS 2–6: Sc in each st around.

RND 7: 2 sc in each st around—10 sc.

RND 8: 2 sc in each st around, turn—20 sc.

Work leaf section back and forth in rows.

ROW 1: Ch 1, sc in next 3 sts, turn leaving rem sts unworked—3 sc.

ROW 2: Ch 1, 2 sc in first st, sc in next st, 2 sc in next st, turn—5 sc.

ROW 3: Ch 1, 2 sc in first st, sc in next 3 sts, 2 sc in next st, turn—7 sc.

ROWS 4–6: Ch 1, sc in each st across, turn.

ROW 7: Ch 1, sc2tog (see Glossary) over first 2 sts, sc in next 3 sts, sc2tog over next 2 sts, turn—5 sts rem.

ROW 8: Ch 1, sc2tog over first 2 sts, sc in next st, sc2tog over next 2 sts, turn—3 sts rem.

ROW 9: Ch 1, sc2tog over first 2 sts, sc in next st, turn—2 sts rem.

ROW 10: Ch 1, sc2tog over rem 2 sts, turn—1 st.

Work leaf edging as foll: Without fastening off, ch 1 and work sc edging around the leaf toward the stem, around the stem, and back up to the tip of the leaf as foll: sc in end of each leaf-row, sc in each st around stem as desired. Fasten off.

All other sizes

With green, ch 2.

RND 1: 5 sc in 2nd ch from hook, pm in first st, do not join—5 sts.

RND 2: Sc in each st around.

RND 3: 2 sc in each st around—10 sts.

RNDS 4–9: Sc in each st around.

RND 10: 2 sc in each st around—20 sts.

RND 11: Sc in each st around, turn.

Work leaf section back and forth in rows.

ROW 1: Ch 1, sc in next 3 sts, turn leaving rem sts unworked—3 sts.

ROW 2: Ch 1, 2 sc in first st, sc in next st, 2 sc in next st, turn—5 sts.

ROW 3: Ch 1, 2 sc in first st, sc in next 3 sts, 2 sc in next st, turn—7 sts.

ROW 4: Ch 1, sc in each st across, turn.

ROW 5: Ch 1, 2 sc in first st, sc in next 5 sts, 2 sc in next st, turn—9 sts.

ROWS 6–8: Ch 1, sc in each st across, turn.

ROW 9: Ch 1, sc2tog (see Glossary) over first 2 sts, sc in next 5 sts, sc2tog over next 2 sts, turn—7 sts rem.

ROW 10: Ch 1, sc in each st across, turn.

ROW 11: Ch 1, sc2tog over first 2 sts, sc in next 3 sts, sc2tog over next 2 sts, turn—5 sts rem.

ROW 12: Ch 1, sc2tog over first 2 sts, sc in next st, sc2tog over next 2 sts, turn—3 sts rem.

ROW 13: Ch 1, sc2tog over first 2 sts, sc in next st, turn—2 sts rem.

ROW 14: Ch 1, sc2tog over rem 2 sts, ch 1—1 st rem. Fasten off.

*With WS facing, join green in 2nd st of stem from last leaf worked, sc in same st and in each of next 2 sts, rep Rows 2–12, fasten off; rep from * for 3 more leaves but do not fasten off final leaf.

Work leaf edging as foll: Beg on final leaf, ch 1 and work sc edging around leaves and stem as foll: sc in end of each leaf-row, (sc, ch 1, sc) in tip of each leaf, sc in each st around stem as desired. Fasten off.

Finishing

Booties

Block leaves by wetting and pinning flat to dry or by carefully ironing flat.

If the booties tend to slip off the baby's wiggly feet, you may wish to weave a length of the yarn in and out between the dc or hdc posts and tie it in a bow at the front of the booties.

Hat

Weave in loose ends. Block leaves flat.

With green yarn threaded on a tapestry needle, sew leaves to top of hat, weave in loose ends.

CHLOE NIGHTINGALE lives in Scotland. Visit her website at www.galvanic.co.uk.

Just Enough BLANKET

by Amy O'Neill Houck

When designer Amy O'Neill Houck's son was a toddler, she found most baby blankets to be too big for a car seat or stroller. She designed this blanket to fit nicely without hanging off the edge of a seat or getting caught in stroller wheels. Worked from the center out with corner increases, the blanket's final dimensions are determined by the length of the foundation chain. Modified filet crochet rounds add textural interest to the multicolored stripe pattern.

Finished Size
18" (45.5 cm) wide and 28" (71 cm) long.

Yarn
Blue Sky Alpacas Skinny Dyed (100% organically grown cotton; 165 yd [150 m]/2.25 oz [65 g]; (3)): #301, glacier (MC), 2 skeins; #303, sprout (CC1), 2 skeins; #310 coffee (CC2), 1 skein.

Hook
Size G/7 (4.5 mm) hook. Adjust hook size if necessary to obtain the correct gauge.

Notions
Yarn needle.

Gauge
14 sts and 9 rows = 4" (10 cm) in dc.

notes

* Blanket is worked from the center out in joined rnds; first work across the foundation ch, then down the back side of the ch. Do not turn after each round. Fasten off previous color when joining new color. Work first dc of each rnd in sp bet first 2 dc of rnd; work the last dc in sp bet last 2 dc of rnd.

stitch guide

Corner inc
(2 dc, ch 2, 2 dc) in same sp or st.

Blanket

With MC, ch 19.

RND 1: (Dc, ch 2, 2 dc) through both lps of 4th ch from hook (counts as first corner inc), dc through both lps of next 14 ch, corner inc (see Stitch Guide) in last ch, corner inc in back side of same ch, dc in bottom ridge lp of next 14 foundation ch, corner inc in back of last ch. With CC1, sl st in 3rd ch of beg ch-3 to join. Fasten off MC (see notes). Do not turn—44 dc (4 dc on each short edge; 18 dc on each long edge).

RND 2: Ch 3 (counts as dc here and throughout), *dc in each st to corner, corner inc in ch-2 sp; rep from * around ending with dc in each dc to end, sl st in 3rd ch of beg ch-3 to join—56 dc (7 dc on each short edge; 21 dc on each long edge).

RNDS 3–4: Rep Rnd 2, joining MC in sl st at end of Rnd 4—80 dc.

RNDS 5–6: Rep Rnd 2, joining CC2 in sl st at end of Rnd 6—104 dc.

RND 7: (FILET RND) Ch 4 (counts as dc, ch 1), sk next dc, dc in next dc, *[ch 1, sk next dc, dc in next dc] to corner, corner inc in ch-2 sp; rep from * around, [ch 1, sk next dc, dc in next dc] to end of rnd, ch 1, using CC1 sl st in 3rd ch of beg ch-4 to join—50 ch-1 sps (9 ch-1 sps on each short edge; 16 ch-1 sps on each long edge).

RND 8: Ch 3, 2 dc in each ch-1 sp to 2 dc before corner, dc in next 2 dc, *corner inc in ch-2 sp, dc in next 2 dc, 2 dc in each ch-1 sp to 2 dc before corner, dc in next 2 dc; rep from * around ending with 2 dc in each ch-1 sp to end of rnd, sl st in 3rd ch of beg ch-3 to join—132 dc (26 dc on each short edge; 40 dc on each long edge).

RND 9: Rep Rnd 2, joining MC in sl st at end of rnd—144 dc.

RNDS 10–13: Rep Rnd 2, joining CC2 in sl st at end of Rnd 13—192 dc.

RND 14: Rep Rnd 7—94 ch-1 sps (20 ch-1 sps on each short edge; 27 ch-1 sps on each long edge).

RND 15: Rep Rnd 8, joining CC1 in sl st at end of rnd—220 dc (48 dc on each short edge; 62 dc on each long edge).

RNDS 16–17: Rep Rnd 2, joining MC in sl st at end of Rnd 17—232 dc.

RNDS 18–19: Rep Rnd 2, joining CC1 in sl st at end of Rnd 19—244 dc.

RNDS 20–21: Rep Rnd 2, joining MC in sl st at end of Rnd 21—256 dc.

RND 22: Rep Rnd 2, joining CC2 in sl st at end of rnd—268 dc.

RND 23: (FILET RND) Ch 4 (counts as dc, ch 1), sk next dc, dc in next dc, *[ch 1, sk next dc, dc in next dc] to corner, corner inc in ch-2 sp, ch 1, dc in next dc; rep from * for each corner, [ch 1, sk next dc, dc in next dc] to end of rnd, ch 1, sl st in 3rd ch of beg ch-4 to join—130 ch-1 sps (29 ch-1 sps on each short edge; 36 ch-1 sps on each long edge).

Fasten off and weave in loose ends. Steam-block lightly to measurements.

AMY O'NEILL HOUCK writes and designs from Cordova, Alaska. She blogs at www.thehookandi.com.

Summer Daisy SUNDRESS

by Lisa Naskrent

Summer blossoms and cotton breezes come together in this enchanting sundress for little garden babies and toddlers. Adjustable ties for straps allow the dress to fit all season long, and the optional ribbon embellishment adds a final touch of whimsy.

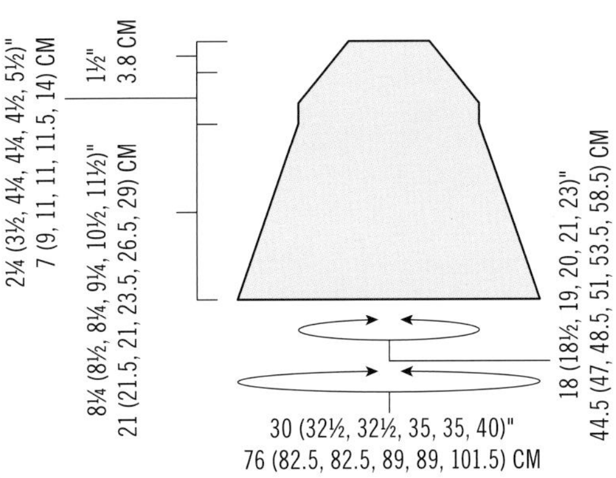

Finished Size
18 (18½, 19, 20, 21, 23)" (45.5 [47, 48.5, 51, 53.5, 58.5] cm) chest circumference, 12½ (13½, 14, 15, 16½, 18½)" (30.5 [34.5, 35.5, 38, 42, 47] cm) length to fit 6 months (9 months, 12 months, 18 months, 24 months, 3T). Garment shown fits 12 months.

Yarn
Tahki Cotton Classic (100% cotton; 108 yd [100 m]/1.75 oz [50 g], (3)): #3353 dark cantaloupe, 5 (5, 5, 6, 6, 7) hanks.

Hook
Size F/5 (3.75 mm). Adjust hook size if necessary to obtain the correct gauge.

Notions
Yarn needle; sewing thread and needle; ⅓ (⅓, ⅓, ½, ½, ½) yd (0.3 [0.3, 0.3, 0.45, 0.45, 0.45] m) of ½" (1.3 cm) wide embellished ribbon; stitch markers (m).

Gauge
8 ch-2 sps and 13 rows = 4" (10 cm) in bodice patt: 1 motif = 1½" (3.8 cm) square.

notes

* Front and back bodice beg with a strip of motifs that are crocheted tog as you go. Each motif consists of 3 top ch-sps and 3 bottom ch-sps of different lengths and will be referred to as such when working panels and neck edging. It is essential to check gauge for both motif and panel patt.

stitch guide

Front post double crochet (FPdc)
Yo, insert hook from front to back to front around post of st and pull up a lp, [yo and draw through 2 lps on hook] 2 times.

Beginning cluster (beg-cl)
Ch 2, [yo, insert hook in st and pull up a lp, yo and draw through 2 lps on hook] 2 times in same st, yo and draw through 3 lps on hook.

Cluster (cl)
[Yo, insert hook in st and pull up a lp, yo and draw through 2 lps on hook] 3 times in same st, yo and draw through 4 lps on hook.

Tie
(Hdc, dc, ch 41, sl st in 2nd ch from hook and in each ch across, dc, hdc) in sp indicated.

Bodice pattern (multiple of 3 ch + 2)
Set-up row: (Sc, ch 2, sc) in 2nd ch from hook, *sk next 2 ch, (sc, ch 2, sc) in next ch; rep from * across, turn.

Row 1: Ch 1, (sc, ch 2, sc) in each ch-2 sp across, turn.

Row 2: Ch 1, (sc, [ch 2, sc] 2 times) in first ch-2 sp, (sc, ch 2, sc) in each ch-2 sp to last ch-2 sp, (sc, [ch 2, sc] 2 times) in last ch-2 sp, turn.

Skirt pattern
Rnd 1: Ch 1, (sc, ch 2, sc) in first 3 ch-2 sps, FPdc around next FPdc, *(sc, ch 2, sc) in next 3 ch-2 sps, FPdc around next FPdc; rep from * around, sl st in first sc to join.

Rnd 2: Ch 1, (sc, ch 2, sc) in first 3ch-2 sps, 2 FPdc around next FPdc, *(sc, ch 2, sc) in next 3 ch-2 sps, 2 FPdc around next FPdc; rep from * around, sl st in first sc to join.

Rnd 3: Ch 1, (sc, ch 2, sc) in first 3 ch-2 sps, FPdc around each FPdc to next ch-2 sp, *(sc, ch 2, sc) in next 3 ch-2 sps, FPdc around each FPdc to next ch-2 sp; rep from * around, sl st in first sc to join.

Rnd 4: Ch 1, (sc, ch 2, sc) in first 3 ch-2 sps, 2 FPdc around next FPdc, FPdc around each FPdc to next ch-2 sp, *(sc, ch 2, sc) in next 3 ch-2 sps, 2 FPdc around next FPdc, FPdc around each FPdc to next ch-2 sp; rep from * around, sl st in first sc to join.

Motif Strip (make 2)

First motif only
Ch 4, sl st in first ch to form ring.

RND 1: (RS) Working in ring, beg-cl (see Stitch Guide), ch 3, [cl (see Stitch Guide), ch 5] 2 times, cl, place marker (pm) in last ch-5 sp made for attaching bodice, ch 3, [cl, ch 5] 2 times, sl st in beg cl to join, pm in last ch-5 sp made for attaching next motif—6 cl. Fasten off.

Motifs 2–3 (2–3, 2–3, 2–4, 2–4, 2–4) only
Ch 4, sl st in first ch to form ring.

RND 1: (RS) Working in ring, beg-cl, ch 3, being careful not to twist motifs, *cl in ring of working motif, ch 2, sc in marked ch-5 sp on WS of last motif made, remove m, ch 2; rep from * once, cl in ring of working motif, ch 3 [cl in ring of working motif, ch 5] 2 times, sl st in top of first

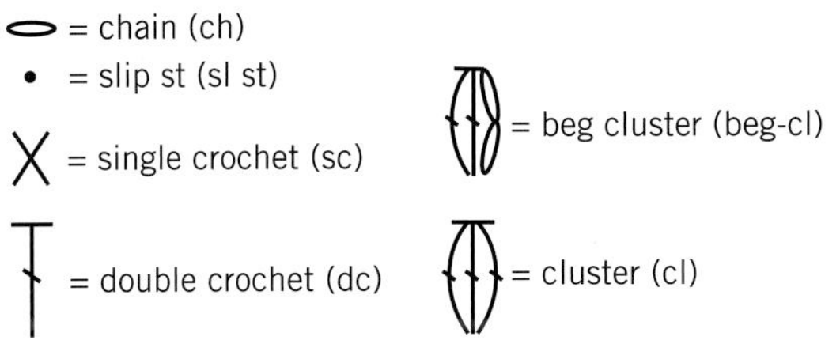

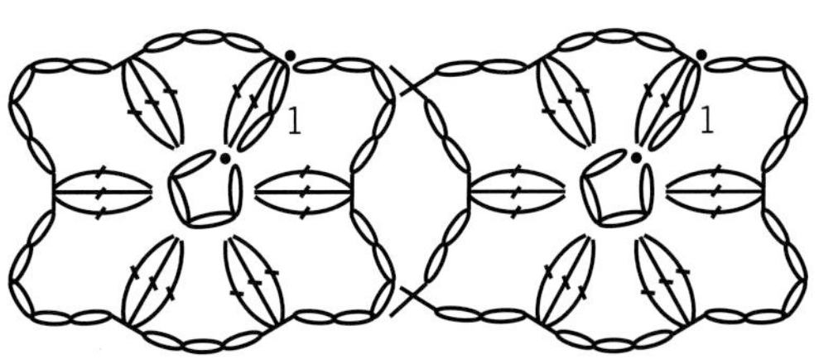

First Motif

Joining of second and successive motifs

cl to join, pm in last ch-5 sp made for attaching next motif (do not pm if this is last motif). Fasten off.

Front and Back Bodice

(rep for each motif strip)

ROW 1: (RS) Ch 3, with RS of one motif strip facing, join chain with sl st in ch-5 sp marked for bodice, ch 1, working in bottom ch-sps (see Notes) across bottom edge of motif strip, work 21 (21, 23, 25, 27, 25) sc evenly across, turn—21 (21, 23, 25, 27, 25) sc.

ROW 2: Ch 4, (sc, ch 2, sc) in 2nd ch from hook, sk next 2 ch, (sc, ch 2, sc) in next sc, *sk next sc, (sc, ch 2, sc) in next sc; rep from * to last 3 ch, sk next 2 ch, (sc, ch 2, sc) in last ch, turn—13 (13, 14, 15, 16, 15) ch-2 sps.

Size 6 months only

ROWS 3–6: Rep Rows 1–2 of bodice patt (see Stitch Guide) 2 times, fasten off if first bodice; if 2nd bodice, turn, cont to Joining Front and Back section (below)—17 ch-2 sps.

Sizes 9 months (12 months, 18 months, 24 months, 3T) only

ROW(S) 3 (3–5, 3–5, 3–5, 3–4): Rep Row 1 of bodice patt (see Stitch Guide) 1 (3, 3, 3, 2) time(s).

ROW 4 (6, 6, 6, 5): Rep Row 2 of bodice patt—15 (16, 17, 18, 17) ch-2 sps.

ROWS 5–8 (7–10, 7–10, 7–10, 6–12): [Rep Row 1 two times and then Row 2 of bodice patt] 1 (1, 1, 1, 2) time(s); rep Row 1 of bodice patt once more, fasten off if first bodice; if 2nd bodice, turn, cont to Joining Front and Back section (below)—17 (18, 19, 20, 21) ch-2 sps.

All sizes

Joining front and back

RND 1: (RS) Ch 1, (sc, ch 2, sc) 1 (2, 1, 1, 1, 1) time(s) in first ch-2 sp, *(sc, ch 2, sc) in each ch-2 sp across bodice to last ch-2 sp, ch 5 (5, 5, 5, 5, 8) for underarm*; working in last row on RS of first bodice, rep from * to * once, being careful not twist bodices, sl st in first sc on RS of 2nd bodice to join—34 (35, 36, 38, 40, 42) ch-2 sps.

RND 2: Ch 1, *(sc, ch 2, sc) in each ch-2 sp to underarm ch, sk next 2 ch, [(sc, ch 2, sc) in next ch, sk next 2 ch] 1 (1, 1, 1, 1, 2) time(s), (sc, ch 2, sc) in next ch-2 sp; rep from * once, sl st in first sc to join—36 (37, 38, 40, 42, 46) ch-2 sps.

RND(S) 3 (3, 3–4, 3–4, 3–5, 3–6): Ch 1, (sc, ch 2, sc) in each ch-2 sp around, sl st in first sc to join, do not fasten off.

Beg skirt

RND 1: Ch 1, work 2 (4, 3, 4, 2, 4) sc in first ch-2 sp, 2 sc in next 17 (17, 18, 19, 20, 22) ch-2 sps, 2 (4, 3, 4, 2, 4) sc in next ch-2 sp, 2 sc in last 17 (18, 18, 19, 20, 22) ch-2 sps, sl st in first sc to join—72 (78, 78, 84, 84, 96) sc.

RND 2: Sk first sc (of join), dc in next sc, working behind dc just made, sc in skipped sc, *sk next sc, dc in next sc, working behind dc just made, sc in skipped sc; rep from * around, sl st in first sc to join—72 (78, 78, 84, 84, 96) sts.

RND 3: Sl st in first sc, ch 1, (sc, ch 2, sc) in same sc, [sk next dc, (sc, ch 2, sc) in next sc] 2 times, dc in next dc, *(sc, ch 2, sc) in next sc, [sk next dc, (sc, ch 2, sc) in next sc] 2 times, dc in next dc; rep from * around working last dc in first sl st, sl st in first sc to join—36 (39, 39, 42, 42, 48) ch-2 sps, 12 (13, 13, 14, 14, 16) dc.

RND 4: Ch 1, (sc, ch 2, sc) in first 3 ch-2 sps, FPdc (see Stitch Guide) around next dc, *(sc, ch 2, sc) in next 3 ch-2 sps, FPdc around next dc; rep from * around, sl st in first sc to join—36 (39, 39, 42, 42, 48) ch-2 sps, 12 (13, 13, 14, 14, 16) FPdc.

Rep Rnd 1 of skirt patt (see Stitch Guide) until work measures 6 (6½, 6½, 7½, 7½, 8½)" (15 [16.5, 16.5, 19, 19, 21.5] cm). Work Rnd 2 of skirt patt once. Work Rnd 3 of skirt patt until work measures 7 (7½, 8½, 9½, 9½, 11)" (18 [19, 21.5, 24, 24, 28] cm). Work Rnd 4 of skirt patt once. Work Rnd 3 of skirt patt until work measures 9 (9½, 10½, 11½, 11½, 13½)" (23 [24, 26.5, 29, 29, 34.5] cm). Rep Rnd 4 of skirt patt once; rep Rnd 3 of skirt patt until work measures 11 (11½, 12½, 13½, 13½, 16)" (28 [29, 31.5, 34.5, 34.5, 40.5] cm); rep Rnd 4 of skirt patt once; rep Rnd 3 of skirt patt until work measures 12½ (13½, 14, 15, 16½, 18½)" (31.5 [34.5, 35.5, 38, 42, 47] cm), do not fasten off.

Skirt edging

RND 1: Ch 1, 2 sc in first ch-2 sp, ch 1, sl st in next ch-2 sp, [ch 3, tr, ch 3, sl st] 3 times in same sp, ch 1, 2 sc in next ch-2 sp, sc in each FPdc to next ch-2 sp, *2 sc in ch-2 sp, ch 1, sl st in next ch-2 sp, [ch 3, tr, ch 3, sl st] 3 times in same sp, ch 1, 2 sc in next ch-2 sp, sc in each FPdc to next ch-2 sp; rep from * around, sl st in first sc to join. Fasten off.

Bodice Edging

With RS facing, join yarn in center ch-2 sp of either underarm, ch 1, sc in same sp, *sc in each row edge up panel, working around motif strip, 3 dc in bottom ch-sp of first motif, 5 sc in first top ch-sp of same motif, work tie (see Stitch Guide) in center ch-sp of same motif, 2 sc in last ch-sp of same motif, [2 sc in first ch-sp of next motif, 3 sc in next ch-sp of same motif, 2 sc in last ch-sp of same motif] 1 (1, 1, 2, 2, 2) time(s), 2 sc in first ch-sp of last motif, work tie in next ch-sp of same motif, 5 sc in last ch-sp of same motif, 3 dc in bottom ch-sp of same motif, 1 sc in each row edge down panel*, 1 sc in ch-2 sp in center of underarm, rep from * to * once, sl st in first sc to join. Fasten off.

Finishing

Weave in loose ends. Cut ribbon in half. With sewing needle and thread, sew embellished ribbon on front and back beneath motif strips and cut off excess.

Abbreviations

beg	begin(s); beginning	**patt(s)**	pattern(s)
bet	between	**pm**	place marker
blo	back loop only	**p**	purl
CC	contrasting color	**rem**	remain(s); remaining
ch	chain	**rep**	repeat; repeating
cm	centimeter(s)	**rev sc**	reverse single crochet
cont	continue(s); continuing	**rnd(s)**	round(s)
dc	double crochet	**RS**	right side
dtr	double treble crochet	**sc**	single crochet
dec(s)('d)	decrease(s); decreasing; decreased	**sk**	skip
est	established	**sl**	slip
fdc	foundation double crochet	**sl st**	slip(ped) stitch
flo	front loop only	**sp(s)**	space(es)
foll	follows; following	**st(s)**	stitch(es)
fsc	foundation single crochet	**tch**	turning chain
g	gram(s)	**tog**	together
hdc	half double crochet	**tr**	treble crochet
inc(s)('d)	increase(s); increasing; increased	**WS**	wrong side
k	knit	**yd**	yard
lp(s)	loop(s)	**yo**	yarn over hook
MC	main color	*****	repeat starting point
m	marker	**( )**	alternate measurements and/or instructions
mm	millimeter(s)	**[ ]**	work bracketed instructions a specified number of times

Standard Yarn Weight System

0 LACE
Yarn: Fingering, 10-count crochet thread
Gauge: 33–40 sts
Hook (metric): 1.5–2.25 mm
Hook (U.S.): 000 to 1

1 SUPERFINE
Yarn: Sock, Fingering, Baby
Gauge: 21–32 sts
Hook (metric): 2.25–3.5 mm
Hook (U.S.): B-1 to E-4

2 FINE
Yarn: Sport, Baby
Gauge: 16–20 sts
Hook (metric): 3.5–4.5 mm
Hook (U.S.): E-4 to G-7

3 LIGHT
Yarn: DK, Light Worsted
Gauge: 12–17 sts
Hook (metric): 3.5–4.5 mm
Hook (U.S.): G-7 to I-9

4 MEDIUM
Yarn: Worsted, Afghan, Aran
Gauge: 11–14 sts
Hook (metric): 5.5–6.5 mm
Hook (U.S.): I-9 to K-10½

5 BULKY
Yarn: Chunky, Craft, Rug
Gauge: 8–11 sts
Hook (metric): 6.5–9 mm
Hook (U.S.): K-10½ to M-13

6 SUPER BULKY
Yarn: Bulky, Roving
Gauge: 5–9 sts
Hook (metric): 9 mm and larger
Hook (U.S.): M-13 and larger

Crochet Gauge

To check gauge, chain 30 to 40 stitches using recommended hook size. Work in pattern stitch until piece measures at least 4" (10 cm) from foundation chain. Lay swatch on flat surface. Place a ruler over swatch and count number of stitches across and number of rows down (including fractions of stitches and rows) in 4" (10 cm). Repeat two or three times on different areas of swatch to confirm measurements. If you have more stitches and rows than called for in instructions, use a larger hook; if you have fewer, use a smaller hook. Repeat until gauge is correct.

Glossary

Learn to Crochet

Chain (ch)

Make a slipknot on hook, *yarn over and draw through loop of slipknot; repeat from * drawing yarn through last loop formed.

Slip Stitch (sl st)

*Insert hook in stitch, yarn over and draw loop through stitch and loop on hook; repeat from *.

Single Crochet (sc)

*Insert hook in stitch, yarn over and pull up loop (**figure 1**), yarn over and draw through both loops on hook (**figure 2**); repeat from *.

FIGURE 1

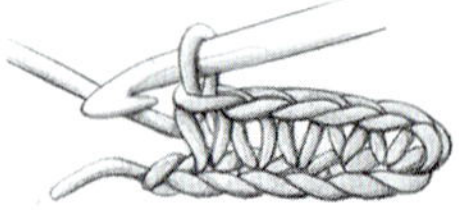

FIGURE 2

Half Double Crochet (hdc)

*Yarn over, insert hook in stitch, yarn over and pull up loop (3 loops on hook), yarn over (**figure 1**) and draw through all loops on hook (**figure 2**); repeat from *.

FIGURE 1

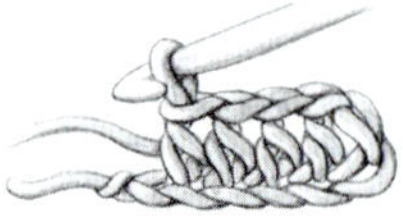

FIGURE 2

Double Crochet (dc)

*Yarn over, insert hook in stitch, yarn over and pull up loop (3 loops on hook; **figure 1**), yarn over and draw through 2 loops (**figure 2**), yarn over and draw through remaining 2 loops (**figure 3**); repeat from *.

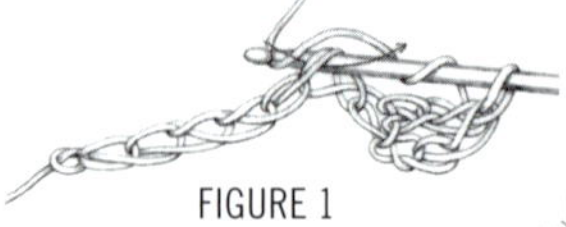

FIGURE 1

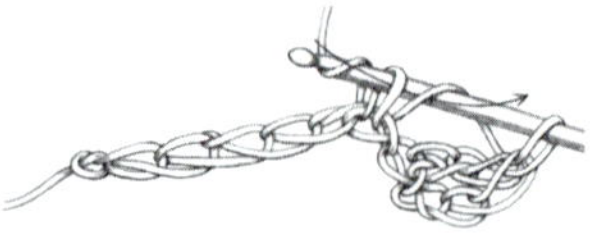

FIGURE 2

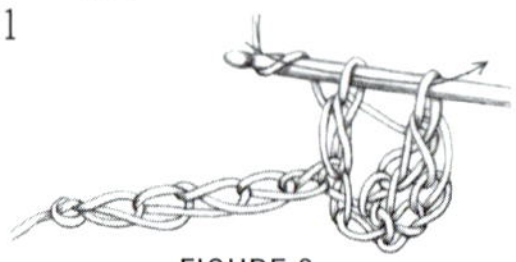

FIGURE 3

Treble Crochet (tr)

*Yarn over 2 times, insert hook in stitch, yarn over and pull up loop (4 loops on hook; **figure 1**), yarn over and draw through 2 loops (**figure 2**), yarn over and draw through 2 loops, yarn over and draw through remaining 2 loops (**figure 3**); repeat from *.

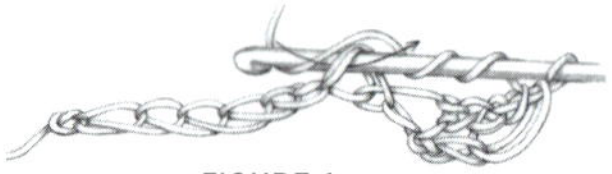

FIGURE 1

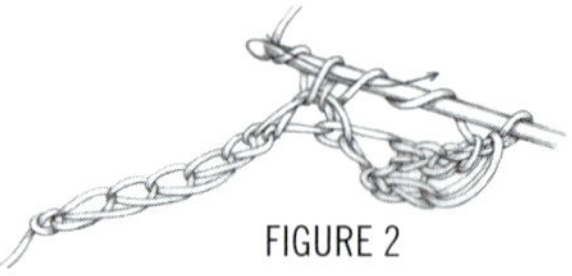

FIGURE 2

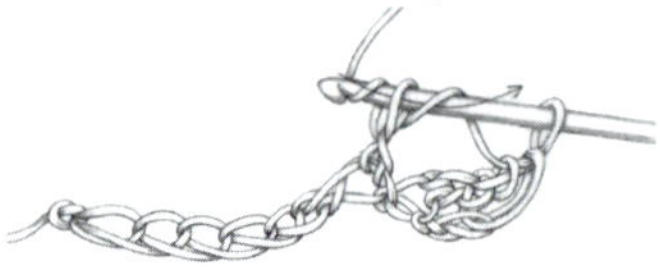

FIGURE 3

Adjustable Loop

Place slipknot on hook, leaving a 4" (10 cm) tail. Wrap tail around fingers to form ring. Work stitches of first round into ring. At end of first round, pull tail to tighten ring.

Adjustable Ring

Make a large loop with the yarn (**figure 1**). Holding the loop with your fingers, insert hook into loop and pull working yarn through loop (**figure 2**). Yarn over hook, pull through loop on hook.

Continue to work indicated number of stitches into loop (**figure 3**; shown in single crochet). Pull on yarn tail to close loop (**figure 4**).

FIGURE 1

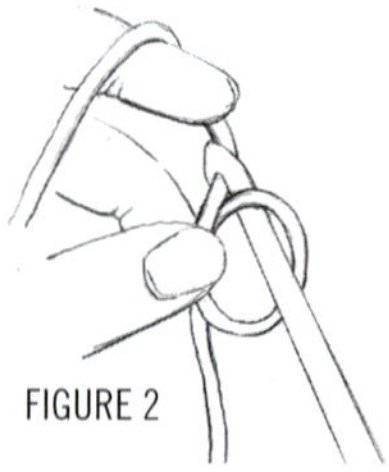

FIGURE 2

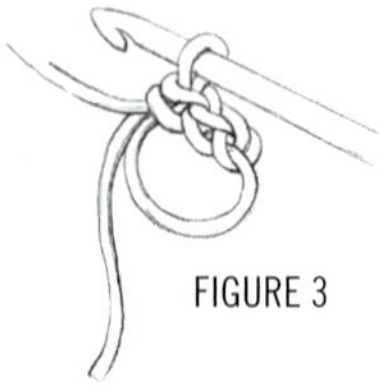

FIGURE 3

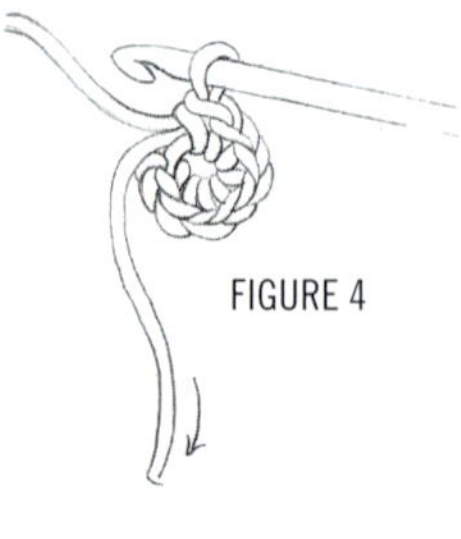

FIGURE 4

Back Loop Only (blo)

Insert the hook between the strands of the "V" and under the loop on the back side of the work. Fabric worked blo has a ridge in it and has more stretch than fabric worked otherwise. It's often used for ribbing.

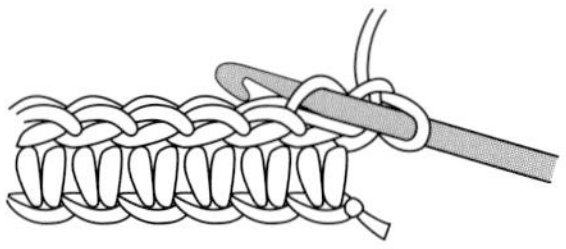

Back Post Double Crochet (BPdc)

Yarn over, insert hook from back to front to back around post of stitch to be worked, yarn over and pull up loop [yarn over, draw through 2 loops on hook] 2 times.

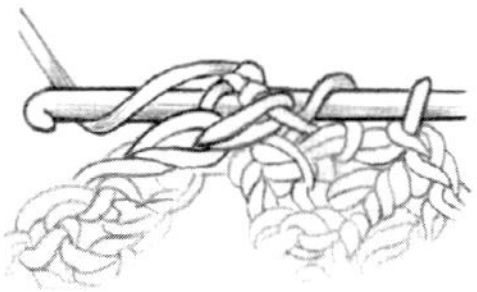

Double Crochet Two Together (dc2tog)

[Yarn over, insert hook in next stitch, yarn over and pull up loop, yarn over and draw through 2 loops] 2 times, yarn over and draw through all loops on hook—1 stitch decreased.

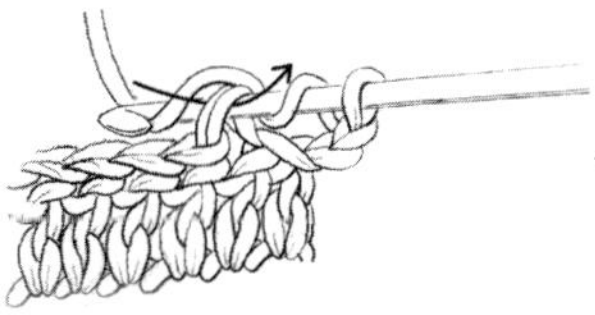

FIGURE 1

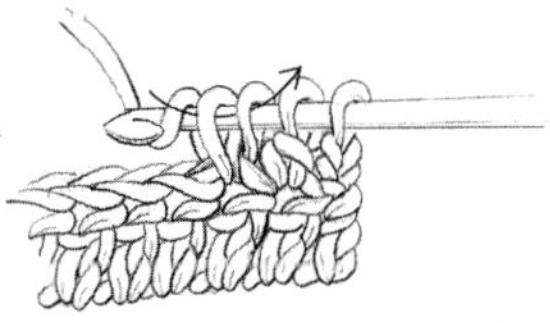

FIGURE 2

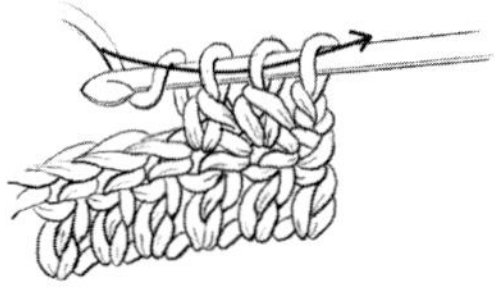

FIGURE 3

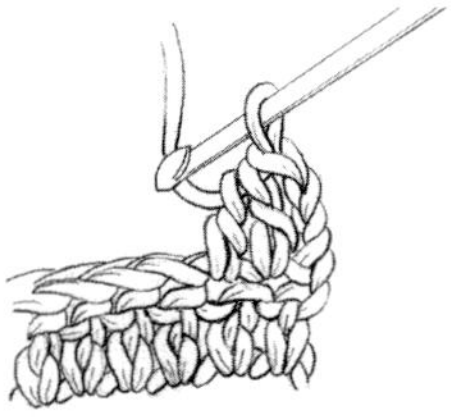

FIGURE 4

Double Crochet Three Together (dc3tog)

[Yarn over, insert hook in next stitch, yarn over and pull up loop, yarn over and draw through 2 loops] 3 times (4 loops on hook), yarn over and draw through all loops on hook—2 stitches decreased.

Double Crochet Four Together (dc4tog)

[Yarn over, insert hook in next stitch, yarn over and pull up loop, yarn over and draw through 2 loops] 4 times, yarn over, draw through all loops on hook—3 stitches decreased.

Front Loop Only (flo)

Insert the hook under the strand of the "V" that is closest to you. Fabric worked flo is flatter and taller than fabric worked otherwise.

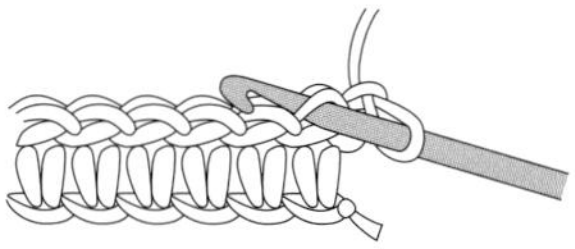

Foundation Single Crochet (fsc)

Ch 2 **(figure 1)**, insert hook in 2nd ch from hook **(figure 2)**, yarn over hook and draw up a loop (2 loops on hook), yarn over hook, draw yarn through first loop on hook **(figure 3)**, yarn over hook and draw through 2 loops on hook **(figure 4)**—1 fsc made **(figure 5)**. *Insert hook under 2 loops of ch made at base of previous stitch **(figure 6)**, yarn over hook and draw up a loop (2 loops on hook), yarn over hook and draw through first loop on hook, yarn over hook and draw through 2 loops on hook **(figure 7)**. Repeat from * for length of foundation.

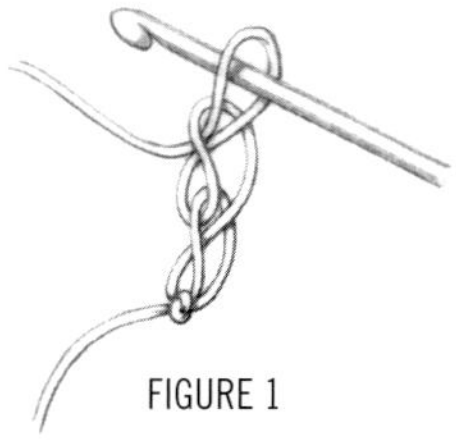

FIGURE 1

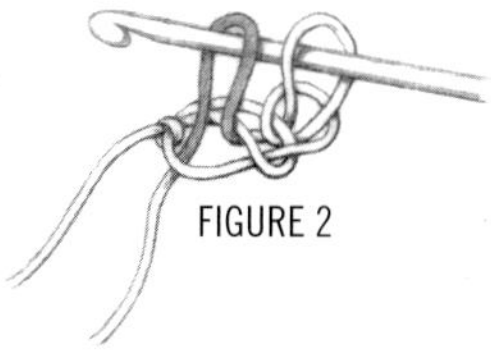

FIGURE 2

FIGURE 3

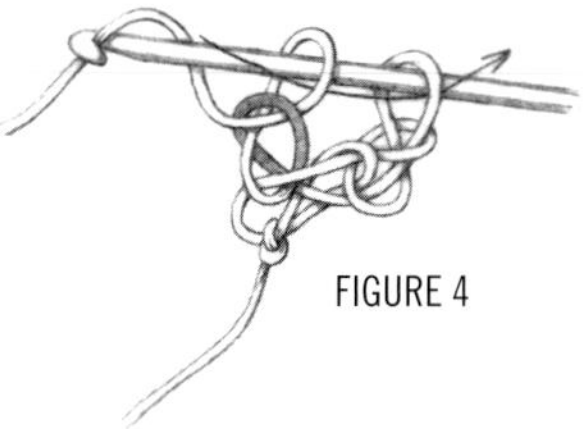

FIGURE 4

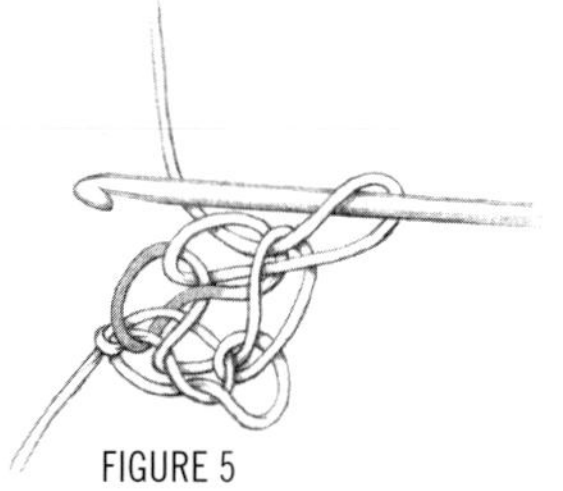

FIGURE 5

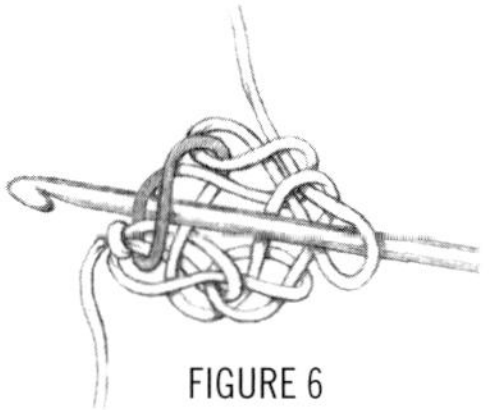

FIGURE 6

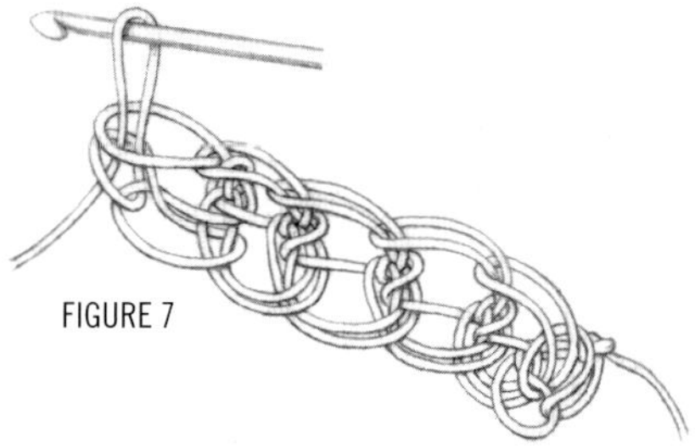

FIGURE 7

Extended Single Crochet (esc)

Insert hook in next stitch or chain, yarn over and pull up loop (2 loops on hook), yarn over and draw through 1 loop (1 chain made), yarn over and pull through 2 loops—1 esc completed.

Foundation Double Crochet (fdc)

Chain 3. Yarn over, insert hook in 3rd chain from hook, yarn over and pull up loop (3 loops on hook), yarn over and draw through 1 loop (1 chain made), [yarn over and draw through 2 loops] 2 times **(figure 1)**—1 foundation double crochet. Yarn over, insert hook under the 2 loops of the chain at the bottom of the stitch just made, yarn over and pull up loop (3 loops on hook) **(figure 2)**, yarn over and draw through 1 loop (1 chain made), [yarn over and draw through 2 loops] 2 times **(figure 3)**. *Yarn over, insert hook under the 2 loops of the chain at the bottom of the stitch just made **(figure 4)**, yarn over and pull up loop (3 loops on hook), yarn over and draw through 1 loop (1 chain made), [yarn over and draw through 2 loops] 2 times. Repeat from * **(figure 5)**.

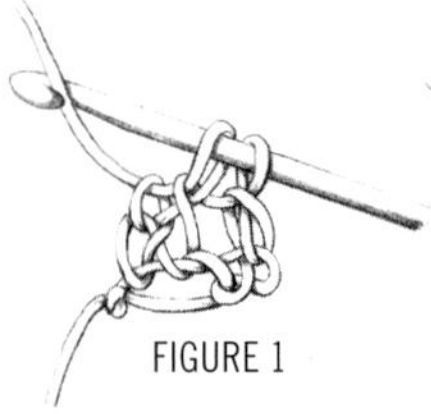
FIGURE 1

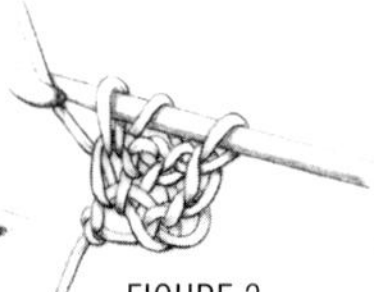
FIGURE 2

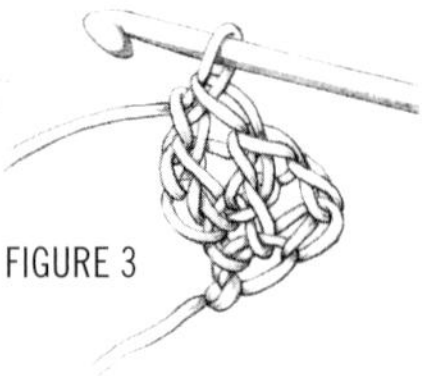
FIGURE 3

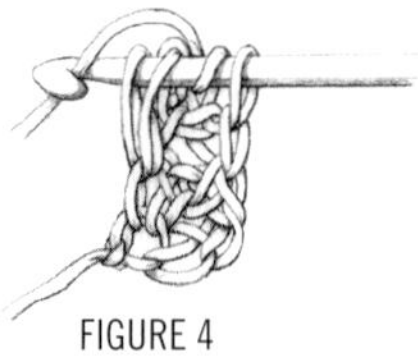
FIGURE 4

FIGURE 5

Front Post Double Crochet (FPdc)

Yarn over, insert hook from front to back to front around post of stitch to be worked, yarn over and pull up loop [yarn over and draw through 2 loops on hook] 2 times.

Front Post Double Treble (FPdtr)

Yarn over 3 times, insert hook from front to back to front around the post of the indicated stitch below, yarn over and pull up loop [yarn over, draw through 2 loops on hook] 4 times.

Front Post Single Crochet (FPsc)

Insert hook from front to back to front around the post of corresponding stitch below, yarn over and pull up loop, yarn over and draw through both loops on hook.

Front Post Treble Crochet (FPtr)

Yarn over 2 times, insert hook from front to back to front around the post of the corresponding stitch below, yarn over and pull up loop [yarn over, draw through 2 loops on hook] 3 times.

Half Double Crochet Two Together (hdc2tog)

[Yarn over, insert hook in next stitch, yarn over and pull up loop] 2 times (5 loops on hook), yarn over and draw through all loops on hook—1 stitch decreased.

Reverse Single Crochet (rev sc)

Working from left to right, insert crochet hook in an edge stitch and pull up loop, yarn over and draw this loop through the first one to join, *insert hook in next stitch to right **(figure 1)**, pull up a loop, yarn over **(figure 2)**, and draw through both loops on hook **(figure 3)**; repeat from *.

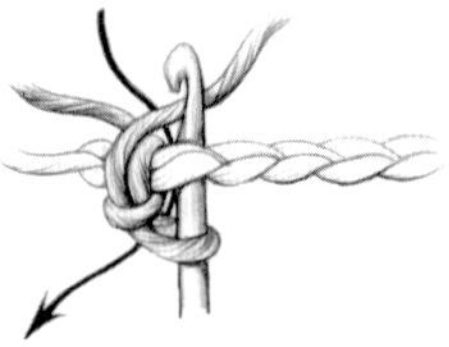
FIGURE 1

FIGURE 2

FIGURE 3

Single Crochet Two Together (sc2tog)

Insert hook into stitch and draw up a loop. Insert hook into next stitch and draw up a loop. Yarn over hook **(figure 1)**. Draw through all 3 loops on hook **(figures 2 and 3)**.

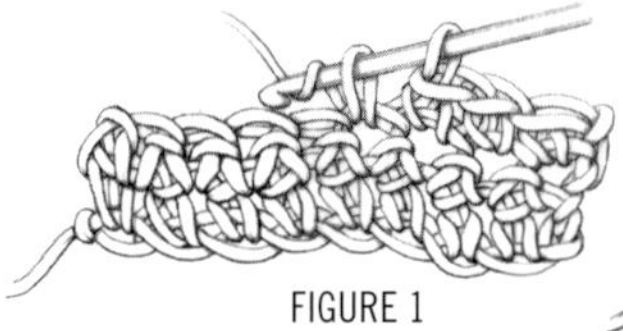
FIGURE 1

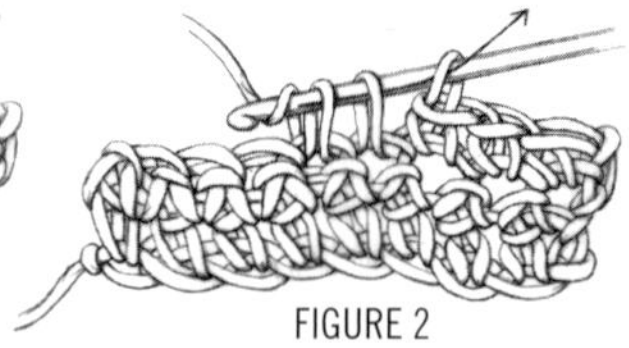
FIGURE 2

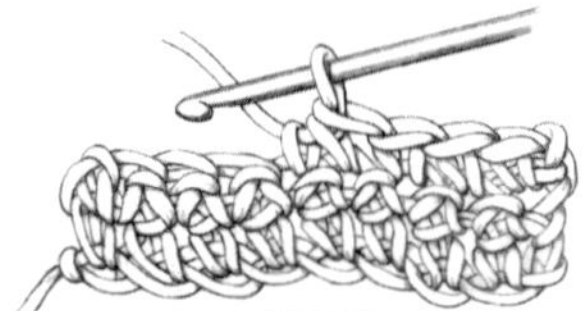
FIGURE 3

Single Crochet Three Together (sc3tog)

[Insert hook in next stitch, yarn over, pull loop through stitch] 3 times (4 loops on hook). Yarn over and draw yarn through all four loops on hook. Completed sc3tog—2 stitches decreased.

Slip-Stitch Crochet Seam

Make a slipknot with seaming yarn and place on hook. With RS of pieces facing each other, *insert hook through both pieces of fabric under the stitch loops, wrap yarn around hook to form a loop **(figure 1)**, and pull loop back through both pieces of fabric and through the loop already on hook **(figure 2)**. Repeat from *, maintaining firm, even tension.

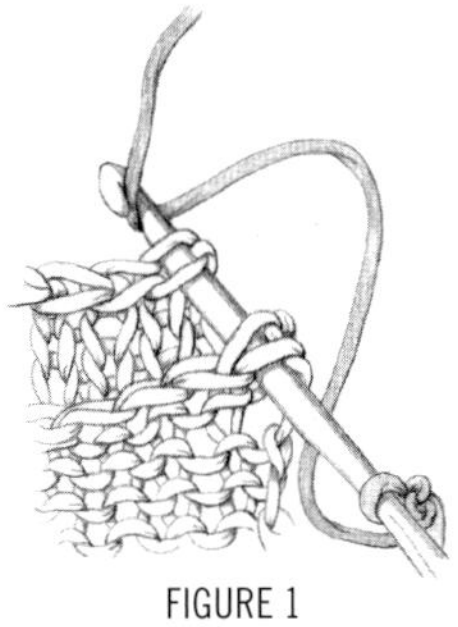

FIGURE 1

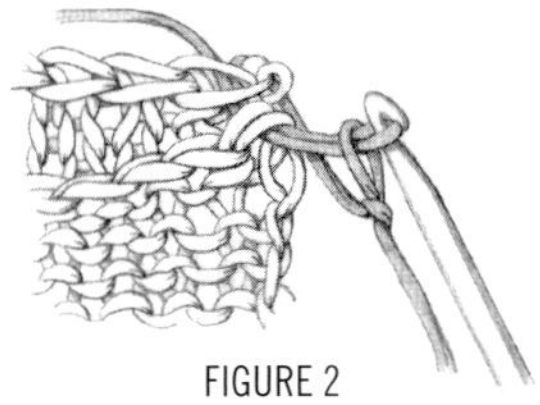

FIGURE 2

Stem Stitch

Bring the needle through the fabric from the back. Take a stitch as shown, keeping the thread below the needle. Repeat. The needle always emerges on the left side of the previous stitch so that the stitches overlap slightly.

Whipstitch Seam

Place pieces with right sides together. Hold pieces with the 2 edges facing you.

STEP 1: Secure seaming yarn on wrong side of one piece. Pass needle through pieces from back to front at start of seam. This creates a small stitch to begin seam.

STEP 2: A little farther left, pass needle through pieces, again from back to front, wrapping seam edge.

Repeat Step 2 to complete seam. Secure end of seaming yarn.

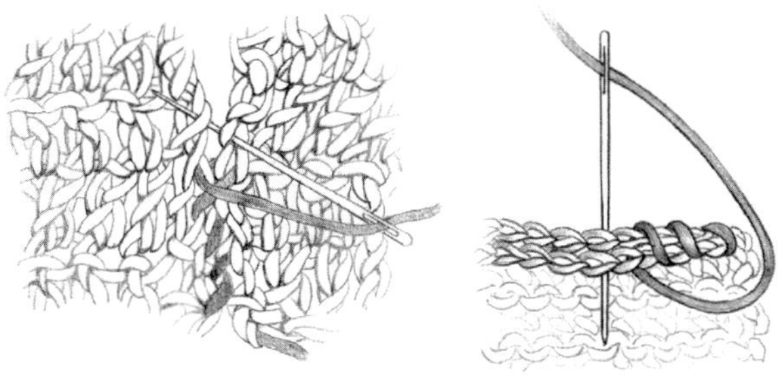

Woven Seam

Place pieces side by side on a flat surface, right sides facing you and the edges lined up row by row or stitch by stitch.

STEP 1: Secure seaming yarn on wrong side of piece A at start of seam. Pass needle to right side at bottom of first stitch.

STEP 2: Put needle through bottom of first stitch of piece B and pass it up to right side again at top of stitch (or in stitch above, if you're working in single crochet).

STEP 3: Put needle through bottom of first stitch of piece A, exactly where you previously passed needle to right side, and bring needle to right side at top of same stitch.

STEP 4: Put needle through piece B where you previously passed needle to right side, and bring needle to right side at the top of same or next stitch.

STEP 5: Put the needle through piece A, where you previously passed needle to right side, and bring needle through to right side at top of stitch.

Repeat Steps 4 and 5, gently tightening seam as you go, being careful not to distort fabric. Allow rows to line up but don't make seam tighter than edges themselves. Edges will roll to the wrong side of work. Secure end of seaming yarn.

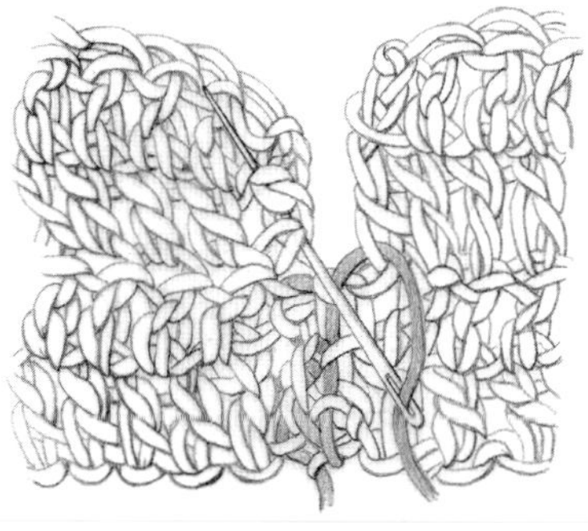

WOVEN SEAM APPLIED "ROW TO ROW"

Find popular patterns for quick and easy projects with these *Craft Tree* publications, brought to you by Interweave.

THESE CRAFT TREE BOOKLETS ONLY $12.99!

Crocheted Afghans
ISBN 978-1-62033-094-4

Crocheted Amigurumi
ISBN 978-1-62033-093-7

Crocheted Baby Gifts
ISBN 978-1-59668-739-4

Easy Crocheted Accessories
ISBN 978-1-59668-738-7

Easy Knitted Accessories
ISBN 978-1-62033-092-0

Easy Knitted Hats
ISBN 978-1-62033-097-5

Visit your favorite retailer or order online at **interweavestore.com**

INTERWEAVE
interweavestore.com